HOMES AND GARDENS BOOK OF Flower Arrangement

KU-176-361

Photographs by
John Miller

GONDOLA

Hamlyn
LONDON · NEW YORK · SYDNEY · TORONTO

HOMES AND GARDENS
BOOK OF

Flower Arrangement

Betty Massingham

ACKNOWLEDGEMENTS

The author is grateful to *Homes and Gardens* for
permission to make use of the superb colour
transparencies reproduced in this book. She is also
grateful to the publishers for permission to quote
extracts from the following books:

The Curious Gardener and *The Contemplative
Gardener* by Jason Hill, published by Faber and
Faber Ltd
The Glass of Fashion by Cecil Beaton, published by
Weidenfeld (Publishers) Ltd
Flowers in House and Garden by Constance Spry,
published by J. M. Dent & Sons Ltd
Home and Garden and *Wood and Garden* by
Gertrude Jekyll, published by Longman Group Ltd

First published in 1976 by
The Hamlyn Publishing Group Limited

First published in 1984 as a Hamlyn Gondola Book by
The Hamlyn Publishing Group Limited
London · New York · Sydney · Toronto
Astronaut House, Feltham, Middlesex, England
© Copyright 1976 The Hamlyn Publishing Group Limited
© Copyright 1984 this edition
All rights reserved. No part of this publication may be
reproduced, stored in a retrieval system, or transmitted,
in any form or by any means, electronic, mechanical,
photocopying, recording or otherwise, without the
permission of The Hamlyn Publishing Group Limited.

ISBN 0 600 34714 1

Filmset in England by Tradespools Limited
in 12 on 16 pt. Monophoto Sabon
Printed in Italy

Contents

Foreword

Readers of *Homes and Gardens* need no introduction to Betty Massingham who, for over twenty-five years, has been giving pleasure in the magazine with her very personal approach to flower arranging. So I address myself now to those who are not familiar with her work.

Betty Massingham was always 'good with flowers', doing arrangements for her parents when a girl at home. Later, as a young woman, her weekly housekeeping budget included three and sixpence for flowers. Her creativity with such modest material delighted her husband and it was he who encouraged her to take a Constance Spry course which was the start of her working life. As well as arranging flowers her career has also included several successful books, lecturing and demonstrating and, of course, journalism.

Though the professional course provided certain skills, it did not alter her feelings about flowers and the way she handles them, which is a more natural approach, using fewer flowers, than that of the traditional professional florist. Her love of flowers led to a great interest in gardening and this in its turn has influenced her work. Plants that look good together in the garden will also blend happily in a vase. She sees her growing plants as a whole, stem, leaves, buds and flowers, and feels that all these elements are important in a floral arrangement. Contrasting foliage, too, she finds fascinating.

Ideas for colour schemes she finds everywhere but the most important source, she says, are paintings. There, in an artist's use of colour, she finds inspiration.

Flower arrangements should never be conceived in isolation. Betty Massingham not only chooses the colours that will enhance a particular room but also ensures that the proportions of the arrangement are in keeping with its surroundings. And that is not all. The character of the flowers must also be in harmony with their setting and the life style of those who live in those rooms.

Develop your own style, she says. Our flowers will then fit in with other manifestations of our taste, the furnishing we choose and the clothes we wear. Then flower arranging – that creative activity available to all – will grow into something entirely personal and an appropriate finishing touch to our homes. It is good advice. And this book with its many beautiful illustrations and its sensitive text, can only increase awareness and give ideas to us all.

Ryche Pirie

EDITOR, HOMES AND GARDENS

Introduction

Although, in this country, the last few decades have seen rapid developments and signs of greater interest in flower arrangement, it may be surprising to find that the early beginnings of cutting flowers for decoration – at this stage rather for garlands than to arrange in vases – may almost certainly derive from the days of Chaucer.

In Holbein's painting of Sir Thomas More's family, about 1530, one of the first known pictures to contain so many flowers, there are three arrangements which include iris, columbines, lilies, carnations and peonies. And so on special occasions, such as for a painting of the family group, flowers were already being cut and put into vases.

One of Queen Elizabeth's courtiers, Sir Hugh Platt, describes in *Delights for Ladies* (1594) a method of drying and preserving cut roses. On the title page of the 1636 edition of Gerard's *Herball* are stylized bunches of flowers in small jars, including fritillaries, lilies, irises, tulips, peonies and roses.

The need for vases must have been felt. Some of the first Leeds wall brackets designed to hold flowers were made in 1745, Staffordshire salt-glazed stoneware brackets date from 1750, and the Wedgwood factory produced their urn-shaped bough pots in 1770.

Allen Ramsay's painting (1754–55) of his second wife includes an earthenware vase holding pink and yellow roses; a painting of Queen Charlotte, about 1770, by Zoffany, includes a vase of delphiniums and roses; and one of her daughter, Princess Elizabeth, by Henry Eldridge, about 1795, shows a small vase of flowers as part of the furnishings for a writing table.

In *The Lady's Country Companion*, published in 1845, Jane Loudon assumes that there will be cut flowers in an English home. She writes on how to enjoy the country including the keeping of gold-fish, parrots and pet monkeys, and some simple rules on how to preserve the life of flowers in vases.

Miss Gertrude Jekyll, one of the great English gardeners, published in 1907 *Flower Decoration in the House*.

Twenty years later came Constance Spry. Perhaps a quotation from *The Times* sums up the importance of her work: 'The essence of her approach was always that one should extract pleasure from the arranging of flowers and her only criterion when judging an exhibit used to be whether it was beautiful or not.'

In the following pages there are some ideas for flower arrangement. I would like to associate my work with words written by Miss Jekyll in 1907: 'In offering some suggestions on the use of flowers in house decorations, the writer is aware how well the matter is already understood in many households.'

Lily Massingham.

Colour and the Flower Arranger

There are so many shades of colours, so many different tones and possible mixtures that, with flowers, the chances of expressing individual taste and planning widely different colour schemes are legion. In the same way this applies to painting, and there are as many possibilities of shades and tones and variations of one colour in a box of oils or water colours as can be found growing in the garden.

The question of colour seems to me to be so bound up with painting, that it is difficult to discuss one without the other.

It can be quite surprising, too, to discover the approach of different people to the same colour. What seems a clear cobalt to one may appear to another to be a greeny blue. There is a vast difference between raw sienna, chrome yellow, and gamboge, but they are all called yellow. It is this variety of interpretation together with the existing subtleties of colour that makes the arranging of flowers as exciting as painting a picture. It is this, too, which makes the description of colour schemes so precarious.

The relation of one colour to another is often what produces a final colour scheme, and makes the description of individual colours so difficult. A well-known painter promised that, if another artist would paint a nude in heavy mud colour, he would guarantee to make it appear pink and opalescent by painting in a certain coloured background.

When thinking in terms of red, pink or crimson, perhaps the flowers which immediately come to mind are roses, carnations and pelargoniums.

Floribunda roses form the main backbone of colour in the large group on the right, Anne Poulsen being an especially suitable one with heavy clusters of flower in scarlet-crimson, Frensham with its wine-red, vigorous and almost continuous flowers and Rosemary Rose with flat, full flowers of bright rose pink with deeper colouring towards the centre. Two useful polygonums are included in this arrangement: *Polygonum affine* Darjeeling Red with thin, deep pink spires and *P. campanulatum* with almost beadlike sprays in pale pink merging almost into white. The first of these is a tough carpeting plant with lance-shaped, fresh-looking green leaves and the second is a wide, branching plant with copper-brown stems which bear smallish, grey-brown leaves. This one seems to enjoy a damp position

A red arrangement composed chiefly of floribunda roses and including some pink-toned flowers. The group is arranged in a white Staffordshire shell vase

for encouraging its continuous flowering through late July into September. A softer pink is introduced by Sweet Williams and bergamot (monarda) and cerise by a Zéphirine Drouhin rose.

There are so many roses, pelargoniums and carnations from which to make a selection – try turning over the pages of a rose book or carnation catalogue. Here are the names of a few varieties of roses especially useful in red or pink arrangements: Anne Poulsen, a good clear red; Garnette, a deep, dark red, very long lasting; Carol, the same small type in a soft pink, also long lasting; Kathleen Ferrier, a bright cerise pink; Betty Uprichard, salmon pink; Queen Elizabeth, excellent for cutting, with strong, long stems and deep pink buds which open into paler pink flowers; Ophelia, one of the loveliest pale pink roses of all, with long stems for cutting; Frensham, a dark red; Dusky Maiden, dark wine red; Moulin Rouge, a flat red; Super Star, with a quality of dazzling brightness, rather garish; Magenta, a soft pink mauve, with full flowers and good foliage; Josephine Bruce, a frequently planted dark velvet red; Rosemary Rose, with flat, full flowers, bright rose pink with deeper colouring towards the centre; and Zéphirine Drouhin, bright cerise pink, wonderful colouring, reliable, long flowering period.

Apart from roses and carnations there are many other pink, red or crimson flowers. *Anemone fulgens*, which is early flowering, comes in a good, clear bright colour; gerberas excel in many shades of red, pink, salmon and rose; geraniums also provide an infinite variety of colour in these shades, and some of the bergamots come in a soft pink as well as the old-fashioned ruby red so often seen in cottage gardens. Camellias, rhododendrons and azaleas are all available in these colours, which range from deep wine through many shades of delightful rose and pink to, in the case of the azaleas, a soft, almost salmon pink.

To describe accurately the various shades and tones of red would probably require a lifetime's study of painting and even then some of the definitions would be difficult. In discussing the colours of red and pink Miss Jekyll, who trained as an artist many years before she became a gardener, wrote: 'It is very easy to say pink, but pink covers a wide range . . . from the tint of a newborn mushroom to that of an ancient brick. One might prepare a range of at least thirty tints, and this number could easily be multiplied, all of which might be called pink; with regard to some room, or object, or flower of any one kind of red, only a few of these will be in friendly accordance, a good number will be in deadly discord, and the remainder more or less out of relation.'

Red is thought of as a cheerful colour. But perhaps we should remember that a small touch of bright red goes a long way, whereas the more subtle shades of pink – such as these columbines (aquilegias) in a wine glass – will fit into almost any colour scheme.

Dahlias, snapdragons, gladioli, geums and zinnias can all make their contribution to a 'red' arrangement in good, strong colours. To

'The prime consideration is transparency, the first characteristic of glass . . .' Laurence Whistler wrote of the use of glass for drawing and engraving, and it is this very characteristic which can be of so much value in the arranging of flowers. The columbines in this wine glass are in various shades of pink

The colour scheme of this small bunch
from the garden is predominantly pink. As
with the columbines, the pink is made up
of various shades and the pearl-white
flowers of polygonum are also included

Dusky rose-pink *Clematis* Comtesse de Bouchaud with dramatically dark and large-flowered Jackmanii Superba and the smaller Etoile Violette give a delicate effect, especially when their twining stems and unopened buds are also included. The only support for these flowers is large-mesh wire netting at the centre of the vase, otherwise the climbing stems support each other. This is a long-lasting group

give a softer touch there are also the entrancing pale pink flowers of *Kalmia latifolia*, the pink-and-white sprays of the evergreen escallonia, Donard Apple Blossom, and the delicate smaller flowers of London pride.

In his classic *The English Flower Garden* (5th Edition, 1897), now edited by Roy Hay in a 1956 publication, William Robinson devoted a good many pages to the clematis. 'I believe these to be the finest of all hardy flowers . . . so graceful is their habit, so bold and showy their flowers, that scarcely a species is without beauty.' For purple arrangements there are certainly few flowers to equal the clematis in variety.

I have often wondered why some people seem to be a little afraid of ordering a clematis for the garden, and in justification have tried to line up the disadvantages of this plant. Perhaps one could say they are a trouble to tie up in the early stages and certainly they are sometimes felled almost down to their base by that disastrous disease known as wilt. If planted close against a wall they may dry out before they are well established, but this applies to almost any plant. These seem to be the only possible criticisms and there are so many blessings that it is difficult to enumerate them all.

First, perhaps, comes the economy of a clematis. For under the sum of £1.50 one can still buy this climbing plant which, once established, will cover in some cases up to 3·5 m (12 ft) of wall or trellis, or rush up a tall tree (as may be seen in the Savill Garden) in a short period of time. Usually there is an over-abundance of flowers which, in almost all clematis, are valuable for cutting for the house and will be found to be long-lasting. I have known certain ones to last for as long as a fortnight.

Then there is the variety of flower shape and colour, and the differences in times of flowering. The many shades of blue and purple are almost too numerous to list but I will mention two of these in the photograph opposite – the dark large-flowered Jackmanii Superba and the smaller profuse-flowering Etoile Violette. Two other popular clematis in these shades are Nelly Moser, pale mauve with deeper pink-purple lines, and Lady Northcliffe in lavender-blue with white stamens which fade into blue.

Clematis are most easily arranged either in Oasis or large-mesh wire netting, crumpled into three layers. I have found that pinholders are not quite as good as either of these – the stems are usually too thin to be fixed firmly.

The charm of the curving sprays may best be seen either when they are arranged in a tall, narrow-necked container, such as a wine bottle, decanter, or an old glass scent bottle (when the shape gives ample support to the stems), or else on a flat dish or plate. In the former case care must be taken to keep the neck of the container well filled up to the brim, as clematis are thirsty plants, and in the case of the latter the water supply must also be watched and carefully checked.

The pale pink of *Clematis montana rubens* is combined here with the deeper pink-mauve of honesty (lunaria) flowers and the purple-blue of the bugle flower, *Ajuga reptans atropurpurea*

Clematis make particularly attractive dining table arrangements, when arranged so that one is able to look down into their flowers and to trace clearly the curves of their stems and tendrils. One method of holding them in position that I have found suitable for dinner or lunch party arrangements (they only had to last in that particular arrangement for a few hours) was to have two or three stems held together in a thimble. The clematis was Comtesse de Bouchaud whose soft lilac and pink colouring I hope to mention again. The flowers were arranged on a long, flat pale purple dish so that the curving stems lay across it. The thimble, fixed in position at one side in lilac-coloured plasticine, held enough water for the three thin stems.

I should like here to include a plea for the wild clematis, known as old man's beard. Its charm, I think, lies in the seedheads and tendrils remaining when it has finished flowering before they have reached the completely furry stage, although I have seen these used to good effect for Christmas decorations with silver honesty.

The seedheads of many garden clematis are often attractive, soft grey-green whorls of methodical tangle, and when this is so they can either provide an unusual addition to an arrangement, or can be the focal point of interest from which the arrangement develops. Seed-heads are surprisingly beautiful earlier on while still silky in texture, although the later, fluffy stage also has its attractions – contrary to expectation the fluffy stage lasts well when cut for decoration and does not, as one might think, fall quickly or blow about the room. It is in fact remarkably tough.

Clematis is invaluable for decoration not only on account of the long-lasting qualities and various colours of certain ones, but because they are not usually available from a florist. It seems sensible, there-fore, to grow them whenever possible.

In the group opposite the chief feature is still a clematis with other flowers in various shades of purple and pink. Mauves, purples, lilacs, wine red and deep blue can all merge together to give an impression of one overall colour, the different tones merely introducing light and shade as with water-colours or oils in a painting.

Different tones of honesty flowers and *Clematis montana rubens* can be a delight in a vase just as much as in the garden. The stiff formation of honesty provides an interesting contrast to the twining habit of the clematis, and the leaves of both make their contribution.

Perhaps this is a colour scheme where the texture and brightness of the container are almost as important as the flowers.

For instance much of the tone would be lost in a black pottery vase with a matt surface. But the lustre teapot, pictured right, helps to reflect the flowers and bring out any available light. The position in the room is also something to be considered; either daylight from a window or the glow of a reading lamp after dark is essential to get the best effect.

Other flowers which would give the same colouring include stocks, iris, hyacinths, bluebells, tulips and polyanthuses at this time of year;

and in the summer there are sweet peas, larkspur, heliotrope (cherry pie), ceanothus and Michaelmas daisies.

I could not write about purple flowers without mentioning violets but these always seem to me to show their beauty best when one or two bunches are put into a glass with their fresh green rounded leaves.

One of the usual difficulties about a blue arrangement is to bring it to life. Blue as a colour is impossible, I think, to define. It varies from dark purple-blue, ultramarine, or deep cobalt, to soft dove grey and palest sky blue. In between these extremes of colour are all the variations to be found when one looks closely into a cornflower or a scilla, a gentian or a forget-me-not, a bluebell or a delphinium.

How is it that these flowers never look lifeless in themselves? I think the answer is simply that there is always some form of contrast – either a coal-black pistil, creamy-white stamens, pinky-mauve outer petals or the shading of a blue petal from quite a deep colour to almost white. An example of this is the scabious with soft grey-blue petals (perhaps the field scabious is slightly more blue than mauve) set off by numbers of stamens, some of them pearl-coloured and some of them off-white.

The contrast of green leaves is something which one is inclined to take for granted, but which has the effect of throwing up the blue tones and giving them a different emphasis. This point reminds me of the occasion when I saw the painting by Jan Van Eyck of the Arnolfini portrait for the first time after it had been cleaned. It was then that the blue and green of the woman's dress made a definite impact, and since that time I have often arranged these two colours together. Delphiniums with hosta foliage or bluebells with wild arum leaves, chimney bellflowers (*Campanula pyramidalis*) with lupin foliage, field scabious with foxglove leaves – any of these suggestions illustrate the point which emerges, that blue often requires another colour in order to bring out the richness of its tones.

Here the delphiniums, many of them still in bud, form a solid background for the wide-open, almost daisylike faces of the scabious and the strange, fairytale shape and colouring of the love-in-a-mist seedpods. But there is the Van Eyck blue in some of the delphinium flowers and his depth of green in the *Fatsia japonica* leaves. And so it is possible with almost identical colouring to produce a variety of groups, either one with stature and dignity or, as shown here, one with rather a feminine lightness. In this arrangement it is the feathery green of the love-in-a-mist seedpods and their accompanying fronds which contribute most to this lightness, especially towards the centre.

The container for this group illustrates the use of white porcelain to give a reflection to the blue flowers, and its shape immediately produces a spreading effect without much difficulty. The flowers and

The soft blues of scabious and some delphiniums are accentuated here by the addition of green foliage and nigella seedheads

19

Three stems of agapanthus with their strap-like leaves of a good clear green look well in a tall, narrow glass vase. When using only a few flower stems an odd number such as one, three or five may be found more artistically correct than an even number

seedheads are arranged in crumpled, large-mesh wire netting held firmly in position by being fixed over the edge of the porcelain in one or two places, concealed by an overhanging leaf, or the stem of a flower.

There are certain decoration schemes and special occasions which demand a blue group.

Weddings and cocktail parties, dances and receptions often impose rather rigid restrictions in the field of colour, and have to be dealt with tactfully. One is told that the bridesmaids are wearing dresses of blue organdie and require the flower decorations to be blue to match them. Or that a dance hall is to be decorated in 'Cambridge blue' or a reception for a film star must be done in blue because the leading lady is wearing an 'ice-blue' dress. A twenty-first party may require blue arrangements as the young woman in question has always thought of blue as her favourite colour. These are all possible reasons for a blue flower group. The same reasons obviously apply to many other colours, but blue may be more difficult than most of them as one is not able to fall back on roses, gladioli, chrysanthemums, or even carnations to any extent, whereas with most other colours these flowers are a safe standby.

Depending on the time of year, there are various possibilities which may be helpful. Delphiniums spring to mind, coming as they do in various heights and in every conceivable tone and shade of blue. If arranged when they are still in bud they will last well. Cornflowers, bluebells, scabious, love-in-a-mist (nigella), hydrangeas, bellflowers, clematis, Californian lilac (ceanothus), globe thistle, hyacinths, iris, larkspur, veronica, monkshood and beard tongues (penstemons) are others which will introduce a lively variety of blues. With certain of these it would be interesting to introduce either two or three madonna lilies, the pale yellow pot marigold (calendula), clove carnations, or a bright Zéphirine Drouhin rose.

A blue arrangement can also be helped by the colour of the container. White vases give a lightness to blue flowers (which they may badly need) or one may try a complete contrast, such as arranging deep blue delphiniums in an orange-coloured container or softer-toned blue scabious in a lemon-yellow vase. Pale blue flowers such as flax or love-in-a-mist can show up well in a lime-green container and the deeper purple-blue of monkshood (aconitum) or larkspur looks attractive and is considerably lightened by copper or brass.

Remember that a blue group will always show up best against backgrounds of yellow or pale lime green or white, and can even look attractive against a clear red, although this tends to give a purple tone to the overall effect. But it is a waste of time putting blue flowers against a darkish ground.

Artificial light is well known to be difficult for blue, and if blue flowers are being arranged specifically for an evening event of some kind it is wise if at all possible to introduce some white or yellow.

The beautiful blue of agapanthus shows up well here against the background of a white curtain. If you can bear to cut them for the house the flowers last exceptionally well. The glass vase stands about 18 in (45 cm) high and provides a good support for the stems and straplike leaves. The paperweights and two stones and a shell give an extra balance to the arrangement as a whole. No anchorage is needed in the glass vase, and the stems showing through seem to me to give an extra interest.

At the turn of the century Mrs Earle, whose book, *Pot-Pourri from a Surrey Garden*, was published in 1898, advocated the use of white paint in houses for bookcases, panelling and woodwork. This must have been something of a revolution at the time, as a great-niece of

Stems of myrtle arranged with white phlox and anaphalis. A white arrangement goes with any colour scheme

Marguerites with their leaves and buds arranged in a white shell

hers remembers the interest she aroused and how unusual it was. Mrs Earle was greatly influenced by William Morris and his *Lectures on Art*, published 1882. The use of white paint was a startling discovery to the late Victorians. There was a time, known as the 'white period', when white flowers on their own, or with only a few leaves, were the fashion. Cecil Beaton described this in his book *The Glass of Fashion*: 'Those who had white rooms considered white flowers a desideratum. The craze for pristine whiteness became so exaggerated that even the green leaves had to be peeled off the branches of white lilacs and peonies. This stripping process, though a lengthy one, produced its surprising metamorphoses, and a bunch of syringa denuded of its leaves became something finely carved out of Japanese ivory.'

Another fashion of a more recent date and of rather a different kind has been the vogue for the white vase. Whether this does, in fact, derive from the 'white period' already mentioned is difficult to decide, but it is true that the fashion for white was not, at that time of the early twenties, confined to flowers. Later Mrs Constance Spry recommended giving the walls of a sitting room coats and coats of whitewash to make a good background for flower arrangements. She first noticed this idea carried out in Tunisia and 'saw afresh the beauty of flowers set against whitewashed walls . . . it certainly gives full and true value to every flower and leaf set against it'. (*Flowers in House and Garden*).

In exactly the same way a white container makes an effective background for most flowers and it is also a way of introducing white into an arrangement. There is an extra emphasis if white flowers are arranged in a white container.

The small photograph shows a white Staffordshire shell – quite a period piece in its way – holding about forty flowers belonging to the *Compositae* family. They are familiarly known as daisies, ox-eye daisies or sometimes as Chaucer's daisy when growing wild, and as marguerites when garden bred. One of the benefits of garden marguerites is that plenty of buds and leaves can be cut to make a solid centrepiece of green against which to show the white daisies.

As to lasting qualities, this is a family which is completely dependable. Marguerites with their sturdy habit might be expected to last well, but the thinner-stemmed field daisies (ox-eye), with a more delicate-looking flower, are even more reliable.

In complete contrast come the dahlias in the large photograph – only five of them and two or three buds. Here they provide a simple dining table group, their whiteness accentuated by the white candlesticks and the small white porcelain saucer. It is so often small touches such as these that contribute to the final effect of the colour scheme, although not seemingly important in themselves. There is no

Right: A few dahlias make a table decoration with white candles and white stones in the water and in the small dish. Here, again, there is an uneven number of flowers

Tall stems of white valerian with their clear green leaves arranged in a green glass jar. The green and white wallpaper and white curtains contribute to the cool effect

doubt that a white arrangement seems to have a certain distinction of its own.

Apart from aesthetic reasons, a white arrangement goes with any colour scheme in any surroundings and with any background. This means that a certain economy can be practised at a time when flowers are scarce and expensive, for a white arrangement can be moved from room to room with confidence.

A white group almost always gives a cool effect, and white flowers mixed with fresh green foliage can be as refreshing on a hot summer's day as a cool drink. Think of madonna lilies, or the single white moon daisies, or lilies of the valley, or Iceberg roses – all give an impression of stillness, calm and serenity, but one must remember that they might tend to give a chilling effect on a cold day in a room without sunlight.

If white flowers are small they give a feeling of lightness and, in the case of Queen Anne's lace and the single philadelphus, have an almost fairylike quality.

What about white flowers with green, grey or yellow foliage?

Solomon's seal (one of the most enchanting of all green plants suitable for flower arrangement) turns the colour scheme into a striking green and white one. The addition of a grey, like lamb's ears (*Stachys lanata*), garden ragwort (*Senecio laxifolius*) or *Senecio cineraria* is most effective and there is something appealing, I think, about white roses with immortelles, or the spiky *Helichrysum angustifolium* with white sweet peas. The foliage of *Convolvulus cneorum* is dark grey-green and goes most attractively with white bluebells or white campanulas.

We have mentioned white flowers with green foliage and the cooling effect that can be obtained by using white and green together. In the photograph opposite there is a large bunch of white valerian (centranthus), but this is not the overall effect. The flowers are arranged with plenty of their own leaves, breaking through the whiteness of the flowers as they mount up the stems in dark, distinct pairs. And then the glass vase is also of dark green and the whole group stands against a piece of green and white wallpaper between white curtains. The general effect, although the arrangement consists of white flowers, is one of green and white.

The white valerian, although unusual and sometimes difficult to find, is worth looking for, as its uses in such a group, quite apart from its attractions (which are many) in the garden, are invaluable. Once established it is easy to keep going as it seeds itself most generously, but it must have good drainage and rather poor soil with plenty of sunlight. As with many plants, if one has time to cut off the first flowers as they die there will be a succession of flowers from this most prolific of summer plants. If cut before coming out into full flower they will last exceptionally well.

Another white flower which has the same pure whiteness as the valerian is the sweet rocket (hesperis), but it is perhaps more difficult to raise. It likes dampness, as well as sun, and has a habit of disappearing during the winter months and not returning in the spring.

One of the most reliable of all white flowers is perhaps the phlox, but it must be cut for an arrangement before it is fully out or it will drop quickly. Like the sweet rocket it cares for a damp situation in the garden. During a hot spell, when the ground dries out later in the summer, the leaves of the phlox will be seen to be among the first to droop down the tall, thin stems, and will only be revived by a heavy

shower or the ministrations of the garden hose with a good soaking.

Some of the most dramatic of all flowers for a white group are, of course, lilies. Arum lilies appear later on and are dealt with more fully in another chapter, but one must mention their value not only for house decoration but also for weddings, church decoration and large social events, where a striking effect is needed.

One of the most important points about a white arrangement is, of course, that the flowers must be absolutely fresh and must never, under any circumstances, be allowed to look faded. This obviously applies to flowers generally, but somehow with white flowers it seems to be even more essential. In the case of the valerian, arranged in a glass jar, it is also necessary to make sure that the water is kept clear and unclouded.

In the minds of most people, I think, yellow is the colour of spring and spring is the time when one hopes for some hours of sunshine after short, cold days of greyness.

This group stands in a round, flat bowl, capable of holding a good supply of water, and the branches are arranged in a stout pinholder which is kept firmly in its position by the use of plasticine. (It is essential with tall stems of flowering shrubs to have the foundation as solid as a rock, or else their height and weight will soon cause the pinholder to slip or even to tip over.) Around and over the pinholder there is a layer of large-mesh wire netting in which the primroses and violets and short stems of hellebores can easily be arranged.

The use of a pinholder may be admirable for stout branches or the wooden stems of chrysanthemums or roses but it will be found that certain flowers with tender stems do not like them, and I would not venture to try to impale the delicate spring flowers such as scillas, snowdrops, primroses, violets or winter aconites upon them. This means, of course, that when two types of stems are being used in one group, as they are here, it may be necessary to consider separately the needs of each.

A piece of wood from a hazel copse and clumps of bright springy moss complete this arrangement, giving it a wider line than would otherwise have been possible, and which is essential to the balance of such tall branches. The moss also acts as camouflage to the wire netting and pinholder, although these are partly concealed by the low group of flowers arranged to the front. The small group of white-and-brown shells at the corner emphasizes the brown of the board with the white painted band along its front. (These are small details which may not at first sight seem to be a necessary part of the whole group but without them the arrangement would have lost something of importance.)

Winter aconites, daffodils, primroses, cowslips, buttercups, forsythia – these are among the flowers of spring and all are yellow. What a difference in shades there can be in this one colour. From the glistening yellow of a buttercup, looking as though it has been varnished in its brightness, one can turn to the more gentle, paler yellow

Yellow is the colour of spring and this group of spring flowers includes daffodils, forsythia, primroses and hellebores

A small bunch of wallflowers introducing the colour of sunshine into an attic room which has been decorated chiefly in white

of primroses growing in a cluster on a mossy bank. Both are yellow and yet these two flowers convey an almost opposite impression – the one of sparkling brightness, the other of a melting, gentle sweetness.

We have probably all seen and appreciated the dramatic effect of bunches and bunches of daffodils arranged on tables down the centre of a long hospital ward or the first clusters of mimosa on the flower barrows reflecting their golden light in wet London pavements. Yellow is nearly always a safe choice when taking or sending flowers as a present. It goes with most colour schemes where red or blue or purple might clash with furnishings – yellow always seems to fit in.

There is nothing quite like a group of yellow flowers to give the illusion of sunlight in a room. In this attic bedroom the effect of these bright yellow wallflowers in a small vase really makes one feel the sun is shining, showing just how much a bunch of flowers can influence the atmosphere in one's home. In some ways one might say that the individual flowers themselves are almost immaterial – it is this quality of their colouring which is so valuable in reproducing the warm, welcome tones of sunshine streaming in through the open window. And, of course, it is not necessary to have vases and vases of flowers – as the photograph shows, one quite small one will do very well. Having emphasized the association of yellow with spring flowers it seems important to mention that the value of this colour does not end there. It goes on, of course, throughout the year and can be depended upon to bring a cheerful note of a sunny day into any room which it adorns.

Here we have a group of summer flowers with much more variety in the colouring – solid yellow and orange in nasturtiums, marigolds and dwarf dahlias, and lightened with a touch of cream. These colours are given extra depth by a few deep purple pansies – again, a lesson learnt from the study of paintings and especially in this case from *Ripe Sunflowers* by van Gogh with its deep Vandyke shadows and streaks of dark red and purple in the background. The well-known *Tulips and Apples* by Cézanne is another instance where shadows of deep aubergine show up the lighter tones of the flowers and leaves. In terms of depth of colour the fruit basket of dark olive brown weave in which the flowers are arranged and the oak table top against which they stand out are two additional factors which will add up in the final effect.

Large-mesh wire netting was crumpled in the glass dish inside the basket as an anchorage, giving the rather low and spreading outline which comes naturally to these flowers.

The warm reds and yellows of nasturtiums, marigolds and dahlias are combined together here with a touch of deep blue to give extra emphasis to their brightness

Flowers for Furnishings and Special Occasions

In the introduction to one of her books Constance Spry emphasized the new feeling that had developed with regard to the place of flowers in interior decoration. She wrote: 'The woman of today takes a personal interest in the adornment of her house . . . having created a background expressive of her own taste she is not satisfied with unrelated flowers. She sees to it that they, too, form part of the whole scheme.'

This book was first published nearly forty years ago, but at the time this was a fairly revolutionary idea and an original line of thought. Until then a vase of flowers had been simply 'a vase of flowers', bearing little, if any, relation to its background.

I wonder if during these years we have really explored all the possibilities of fitting a flower arrangement into a furnishing scheme so that it becomes an integral part of its surroundings? This whole question is a serious one, not to be ignored if the best results are to be obtained.

We know that flowers can look attractive standing alone against three white walls as they are arranged sometimes at a show or for a photograph, with a plain background and foreground but nothing else in the picture. In such cases, this obviously is of necessity: the cost of arranging furnishings, either for an exhibition or a photograph, may well put anything else out of the question. One can admire and appreciate an arrangement under these conditions, but to my mind nearly half its value is lost.

For example, a woman's scarlet hat can look exciting on a model, or a bright yellow umbrella can seem attractive in a shop window, but neither is of any value to someone they do not suit or with whose colour scheme they clash.

Half the value of a flower arrangement is that it should fit into its position. Perhaps a colour in a room should be repeated or picked up, or emphasis should be provided where it is needed; both the height and size of the arrangement should be suitable for its surroundings.

Obviously very different types and sizes of flowers or leaves would be needed for a mantelpiece, a low table, and a wall bracket. Whether the arrangement is to have a light or dark background may also help to determine the colour of both the flowers and the container. Only a bold arrangement (see opposite photograph) could stand out against a striped wallpaper and a porcelain display cupboard.

It is also possible to concede that, carefully placed, an arrangement

This large mixed group, which includes roses, statice, sweet peas, fuchsias and nicotianas, is given the height of a pedestal by standing the vase on a small table

A small group suitable for a reading table made up of a favourite flower – nigella, or love-in-a-mist

may accentuate something of special interest in the room. A particular painting, for example, may be complemented by a vase of flowers if the flowers are chosen so that they pick up a colour in the picture, and do not detract from it in any way. The subject of the painting is important, too: obviously a flower painting does not need further emphasis from fresh flowers.

An example of linking a flower arrangement with a painting comes to mind in the work of Barnett Freedman. A lithograph in his typical colouring of warm coppery red, with blue-green, clear yellow and dark aubergine was the starting point for a group of blue-green hydrangeas with branches of copper and deep purple berberis and yellow roses. This picking out of a colour might equally apply to a lampshade, a cushion or the colours in an oriental rug. I have seen the white fringe on a striped curtain hanging against a dark green wallpaper picked up and accentuated by white campanulas.

Having worked out a colour scheme and chosen the arrangement's position with as much care as possible as to lighting, freedom from draughts, and so on, the shape, colour and period of the container must also be considered. Its shape and colour depend sometimes on the choice of flowers to be arranged, but if the container is right for its place in the room it will also be a valuable guide to the flowers suitable for that position.

Plain vases are selected most generally, perhaps, though some of the earlier English porcelain bowls and vases, such as Rockingham, Staffordshire, Leeds or Chelsea, can be delightful.

Some furnishing schemes demand the introduction of warm colours while others cry out for cool effects. Interior decorators may illustrate their ideas sometimes by paying extra attention to one upholstered chair – let us say a button-backed Victorian armchair covered in primrose yellow material, standing in a key position in the room – or by a small collection of coloured glass – deep Bristol blue, for instance, arranged on narrow shelves with special lighting; or a few French Lunéville dinner plates on a dresser against William Morris wallpaper (in green) or, again, a collection of plain satin cushions in bright marigold, nut brown, cream and silver grey thrown together on a settee covered in dark seaweed-coloured tweed.

In the arrangement opposite I used white and blue flowers, with green seed heads and foliage, all with a delicate shape and appealing lightness: I frequently find ideas for flower arrangements come from the colours used in favourite paintings, and this love-in-a-mist colour scheme coincides with that used by Monet in the *Water Lilies*. The effect is cool and refreshing.

As various tones of colour may be introduced into a room by flowers, especially by arranging a variety of shades of only one particular plant, it may be as well to consider the needs of a furnishing scheme when planting one's garden. This is why I sow a packet of love-in-a-mist seeds as ground cover amongst the roses. The colours are just right for the wallpaper in our sitting room. It seems to me so

sensible to grow flowers or shrubs which are the perfect colour for one's indoor decorations. After all, if they are attractive enough to have on the dining table or in the hall or sitting room, they must be the kind of flowers which would look good in the garden. For instance, I like to have *Kalmia latifolia* growing outside just as much as I like to see a few sprays of its enchanting pink, crimpled flowers in a white vase or a wineglass in the sitting room. With regard to roses, I like to have Madame Alfred Carrière and Iceberg for table decorations, and Stanwell Perpetual, Madame Pierre Oger and the Banksian rose (amongst others) for cutting and bringing into the house for the sheer pleasure of seeing two or three of them close at hand.

In the case of the Banksian rose, once it has started to grow well, one can expect to cut long branches for a reasonably tall group, as shown in the photograph opposite. It likes to grow in a sheltered position, preferably against a warm, sunny wall, and I always understood that it disliked pruning. However, the founder of the Rose Show in this country, Dean Hole, wrote in 1869 in *A Book About Roses* that it should be pruned in late summer after flowering.

My own Banksian rose, planted on a west-facing wall, has found its way round the corner of the house to face south, where it flowers in such profusion that the foliage is scarcely visible. As it has no thorns it is particularly easy to arrange, but if height is needed it may be helpful to raise the wire netting above the vase to give extra support.

There are many suggestions one could make for various colour schemes, such as having a sealing-wax coloured tulip to decorate a room with lime green walls, or the valuable *Alchemilla mollis* both for its flowers and very beautiful leaves. Japanese anemones would be planted for a cool group against a grey wall, anaphalis for its willing co-operation with other flowers or foliage, or *Choisya ternata* for its green leaves throughout the winter, looking fresh and pretty in a white cornucopia. Everyone will have their own personal selection for planting, and one can only make suggestions, but I think it will be found that to bear indoor colour schemes in mind when selecting plants may prove to be helpful and also exciting.

Just as, in a painting, the background colour can show up, intensify or minimize the central group or figure, so a background to a vase of flowers can fulfil the same function. But, you may say, that is all very well with a painting where another tube of paint may be tried out without ruining the whole picture, but one cannot change a certain wallpaper or alter the whole conception of furnishings just to suit a vase of flowers.

I expect we would all agree that some decorating colours are safe for most flowers. Of all these perhaps white is the most certain of success, but we should also bear in mind the benefits of a plain soft background colour such as grey, celadon green or dark blue – all these can be most suitable.

A fireplace can make a handsome frame to a group of fresh flowers

A few branches cut from a flourishing climbing Banksian rose. The colour of the flowers is a deep primrose yellow and the leaves are a fresh green. This is a thornless rose and so is especially suitable for arrangement

and branches once fires are ended. There is a good selection of colours and shapes in foliage available well into the autumn without necessarily having to depend on quantities of flowers.

Quite a small garden can provide colour, texture and shape – at least a dozen different shapes and probably double that number of shades and tones of the basic green and white. None of the plants in the photograph opposite is especially rare or difficult to grow, nor are large quantities required. Others which come to mind, though not included here, are hydrangea, white petunias, snapdragons (antirrhinums), Iceberg roses, green spikes of bells of Ireland and mignonette.

The fireplace surround gave a lead and the inclusion of white was an obvious choice. When there is a guiding decoration colour, it can be most helpful in making the final selection. It is common sense to have light flowers against a dark background, but not always so easy to decide on a colour scheme to suit an area that may not generally have a flower arrangement.

The choice of a container is always important from the point of view of colour but also in this case on account of its capacity to hold plenty of water. It would be useless to try to keep such a large group fresh for any length of time without an adequate water supply. This container is of heavy iron, firm as a rock and holds quarts of water without difficulty.

The first branches to go in were soft grey-petalled stems of *Helichrysum petiolatum* to give width at the sides. I have often grown this plant but do not recall having used it for decoration before. Other grey-foliaged plants included one of the curry plants, as well as the blue-green of *Ruta graveolens* Jackman's Blue and tall stems of the white-flowered anaphalis.

The ruta (or rue) has a strong scent which some people dislike, but placed at some distance, as in the present group, it should be safe enough. Giving additional height to the anaphalis is a spike of sweet corn. Not only are these flower spikes useful but the formation of the leaves on the tall, stout stem is unique: outstanding when used alone.

A cluster of deep wine-coloured leaves next to the anaphalis comes from the purple-leaved variety of the shrub *Cotinus coggygria*. I find this of great value in providing the dark aubergine depth of tone which helps to throw the lighter shades into relief.

Another interesting shrub for foliage and flowers is *Choisya ternata*, here arranged in the centre against the brim of the white container. Its dark shining leaves, forming a neat and orderly background for its delightful white flowers, contrasts with the paler green of the flowers and foliage of the trailing love-lies-bleeding (*Amaranthus caudatus*).

I wanted the globe artichoke for its depth of colouring and the soft blue-green of its outer bracts, as well as the acanthus flower spike.

More clusters of the anaphalis might have been enough to emphasize the white surround, but it is always difficult to leave out a

A summer group to fill an empty fireplace. The colours of the flowers and foliage are selected to follow the lines of the decorating scheme. The rue foliage picks up the wall colouring and the white flowers (stocks, dahlias, Japanese anemones, anaphalis) together with the globe artichoke, the sweet corn, acanthus and *Cotinus coggygria* emphasize the surrounds of the mantelpiece

Queen Anne's lace is arranged here in a green bulb glass, making a suitable group for a small side table. The lightness of the flowers is complemented by the deep colour of the vase

favourite flower (in this case, Japanese anemones) and once included, the others followed – shasta daisies, dahlias, stock, nicotianas, zinnias.

It is, I think, interesting to realize that this appreciation of white came originally as a revolt against the heavy furnishings and dark backgrounds of the late Victorians. People longed for simple, light furnishing colours and when William Morris filled his shop window in Oxford Street with such revolutionary ideas they queued up to get a glimpse, so great was the interest in them. Mrs T. W. Earle, an ardent follower of Morris's ideas, advocated the use of white for paintwork long before it had been thought of – on the stairs, for bedroom floors, windows, etc., and especially for bookshelves and walls. 'I think everything looks well against a white wall . . .' she wrote. She went on to make an interesting suggestion, based on the use of tapestry in the Middle Ages: '. . . in a white room a small piece of drapery . . . or even a few yards of very superior paper may be put in one place – between windows, over a chimneypiece, above a table or under a bookcase.'

Mrs Earle has stated the case for a white wall or room but other colours can also be considered.

A pale clear green shows up equally well white flowers (campanulas), a blue and yellow group consisting chiefly of delphinium and thalictrum, or the cheerful reds and pinks of Sweet Williams.

Grey is an especially helpful background colour and primrose yellow or white are both good in contrast. But here much depends on the shade of grey. A silver grey will take clear colours (the large single poppies, for example) but a dark rain-cloud type of grey may be too heavy and combines better either with a sugar-candy pink (Doris pinks) or else a deep wine (some of the tones found in zinnias or Michaelmas daisies). In the photograph the chair provides a good grey background for the flowers, lightened by the white of the container. The grey in this case is velvet and has a silvery sheen which combines happily with the pink of London pride, the columbines (aquilegias) and the polygonum. Perhaps without the white vase the effect might not be quite so cheerful.

Blue is variable, depending much on the tone. It can be very good. It can be disastrous. In colour photography we usually find that a darkish sky blue is almost infallible.

In our own sitting-room at home we have a dark blue plain wallpaper and it is surprising how many colours show up well against it, especially white. This background is also good for roses. The shocking pink of the Zéphirine Drouhin rose, the deep wine red of Magenta, the delicate pink of Celeste, the almost off-white of Stanwell Perpetual, the cream-white and apricot colouring of Penelope and the clear yellow of *Rosa hugonis* – the solid blue background seems to be sympathetic to them all. Coral is also a good colour in this context and I am always tempted by two or three sprays of *Euphorbia fulgens* whenever they come on the market, especially when arranged with branches of eucalyptus.

'The prime consideration is transparency, the first characteristic of glass . . .' Laurence Whistler is writing of the use of glass for drawing and engraving, and it is this 'first characteristic of glass' which is of so much value also in arranging flowers. In fact, looking at flowers in a glass vase, where the beauty and soft colouring of the stems are to be seen as much as the flowers and leaves, it almost makes one wonder

Another small arrangement for a similar position to the photograph opposite but here the colouring of the flowers is selected carefully to tone in with the velvet of the chair back

how they must look in porcelain or copper or other solid materials where the stems end at the rim of the vase.

Perhaps the charm of transparency is chiefly evident where the stems or branches take on interesting colours, which may not always be obvious at first glance. For instance, when picking primroses from a grassy bank it may be the clear yellow flower which first attracts attention, but on looking closer the slightly pinkish tinge in the stem will be seen to have an appeal of its own. This looks pretty showing through glass.

Having sung the praises of glass with especial emphasis on the charm of its transparency I must now add a word or two of caution regarding the drawbacks which may be encountered. The first of these is the freshness of the water: it must be as clear as crystal to produce the best effect. With certain flowers and branches this may involve changing the water more frequently than would otherwise be necessary.

Sometimes branches arranged in a glass container are difficult to anchor steadily owing to their weight and rather wide stems. It is important to ensure that they are firmly in position as each one is put in before any further material is added. If they begin to slip the whole arrangement will be in danger of collapse.

There are a few simple points to consider when leaves are being arranged either individually or on branches. In the case of branches their shape and outline obviously are important. To find out how a branch will look its best it may help sometimes to hold it out in the position, as far as possible, in which it grew on the tree. Arranged in that natural way it does not then have to assume a false direction. These branches of japonica are especially suitable for an arrangement of this kind owing to the interesting shapes of their stems.

There is some variety of thought about the proper name for japonica. Miles Hadfield, in his book *One Man's Garden*, went into this matter at some length, explaining the stages of nomenclature from Japanese quince or *Cydonia japonica* to *Chaenomeles speciosa*, but reassured us that japonica is 'recognized universally by gardeners and non-gardeners'.

The situation of this vase is a good example of an arrangement which is better done where it is finally going to stand, with the branches curving outward, the width and height of the group designed to fit into a corner or on a windowsill. A note of colour contrast is introduced here not by some furnishing detail but by the blue glass container.

Foliage and branches have gone through various stages of use and importance in arrangements for interior decoration. The Victorians thought of foliage as an accessory to flowers and depended on a few well-tried plants. Shirley Hibberd, writing in 1856, complained that:

Only a small arrangement is needed here, otherwise light would be excluded, but the colours of the japonica and the vase emphasize the furnishing scheme

'The common fault of flowers in vases is that they are bunched . . . too much is thought of colour and too little of leaves.' At about this time Sir Josiah Conder's *Theory of Japanese Flower Arrangement* was published in this country. 'The foliage of flowers and evergreen and other trees is much used in *floral* composition, the arrangement often being without a single blossom.'

William Robinson, also well known for his introduction of the herbaceous border (especially as the creator of the famous one at Hampton Court), was an advocate of Japanese ideas. He comments on the Japanese appreciation of form and line 'in a single twig or branch, with its natural habit shown, apart from any beauty and form or colour of its flowers.'

Here we have the seeds of ideas for using foliage in flower arrangement and during the last sixty years these ideas have crystallized so that today the shape and colour of leaves may be regarded as a fascinating and serious study. It follows that the planting of gardens should be influenced by these ideas and that a knowledge of the various shrubs and trees and plants with distinctive foliage would be helpful to the flower arranger. Incidentally, this bears out an important rule of Japanese arrangement which allows the use of material only when the arranger knows the name and habit of the plant.

A small bowl of flowers or foliage on an occasional table not only affords a welcome but can also be a point of emphasis in a room's colour scheme. I have tried to illustrate this in the preceding three photographs by a vase of flowers and now hope to do the same here using chiefly leaves.

Although this is only quite a small bunch of leaves there is a certain variety of colour and shape. Stems of bursting dogwood with sweet-smelling green spires of *Tellima grandiflora* both give height and a slender contrast to the heavier leaves, especially the dark purple of *Cotinus coggygria*. But the main content of the vase is made up of hosta leaves.

Hostas or funkias or plantain lilies were brought to England from China in 1790 but most of the hostas now growing in European gardens are descended from those brought to Europe by Siebold from Japan in 1830. This is a valuable family both for contrast in the garden and for indoor decoration, where it always seems to last well. Examples of it may be seen in many of the gardens open to the public. Frequently these will be *Hosta undulata*, *H. fortunei*, *H. crispula* or *H. sieboldiana*.

Towards the centre of the hosta group are a few epimedium leaves, heart-shaped, mottled and patterned as they are good enough to become if planted in full sun. Left in a shady position they are usually just a plain green. They have enchanting small yellow flowers which resemble delicate spires.

A summer wedding in a marquee – how many must be arranged every year! But it is sometimes hard to make a decision about suitable flowers since the selection is so comprehensive at this season.

A bunch of various leaves from the garden together with the green flowers of *Tellima grandiflora* arranged in a small copper container. Again, for a window position it is important to choose colours and shapes which do not take up too much light

The rather definite colouring of cornflower blue, white and green provide a contrast to the delicate yellow and white of the striped wedding marquee

Decorating a marquee is usually more difficult than doing arrangements for the house because there is seldom anything to act as a guide in the way of colour or choice of vases. However, in our case, a lead was given by the yellow and white lining material used for the marquee.

The position of a group or groups of floral decoration is a matter for some thought. More than likely the guests in a marquee will be standing and so the flowers must be visible at eye level. A pedestal vase on the buffet table may well provide the solution.

Instead of using lilies, carnations, early roses, eremurus and so on it can be a good idea to try out something simple. For instance, an unusual note would be the use of nothing but Queen Anne's lace. In a large city church the quantity needed would, of course, involve arrangers in hours of cutting, careful packing and transportation, followed by standing the stems in full buckets of water and snipping off small side shoots to give strength to the main stems. The use of simple materials often entails greater effort than more sophisticated flowers.

For our group illustrated here, the bride particularly asked for deep blue cornflowers because they were her father's favourite flowers. Their rather stocky heads and firm, straight stalks seemed to suggest a second flower with a softer outline and more curving stem. Looking round the countryside, ox-eye daisies appeared to be the answer, especially since the bride also wanted white flowers with a touch of yellow to link with the marquee.

The cornflowers, of which we needed a large quantity for both church and reception, came from Covent Garden market. The daisies were located growing wild in the country.

The bigger pedestal dish in which they were arranged with a few sprays of variegated ivy is part of a dessert service. It is deep enough to hold plenty of water, and the flowers are kept in position by two or three layers of large-mesh wire netting. The stems were cut to different lengths, then the daisies were arranged so that their yellow centres could be seen.

Such a group takes time to arrange. Any stem which has a definite curve should be put into a vase at the angle which suits it best to form the main outline. Towards the centre a concentrated effect of colour and shape can be obtained by cutting stems quite short.

The small table to hold the cake is decorated in the colours of the marquee. Where each loop of ribbon ends, a posy of flowers is arranged in a water-absorbent plastic material set in a small dish. The slim vase on top of the cake repeats the theme.

It may not be possible to put up a marquee long beforehand, in which case it might help to arrange flowers elsewhere and leave them ready to be carried in.

We should turn to the United States, perhaps, for ideas for flowers arranged especially to mark an anniversary – any anniversary. There are many important occasions in the American calendar for celebration, including St Valentine's day, Washington's birthday, Thanks-

The marguerites, cornflowers and variegated ivy are arranged here in a pedestal cake stand to give some height as well as width for the wedding buffet table

giving, together with weddings, birthdays and church celebrations. The American authors of *The Complete Book of Flower Arrangement* – Mrs E. C. Grayson and Mr T. T. Rockwell – devote pages of illustrations to suitable arrangements for such occasions, and it is interesting to notice the emphasis in all cases on two points – good taste and originality.

In my own opinion the first of these is more important than the second. Being original can sometimes be a trap leading towards bad taste if it is originality for its own sake which is being portrayed. Good taste is essential always, and the basis of good taste is often simplicity. As the Japanese discovered hundreds of years ago, a good effect can be obtained with simple material and twenty flowers are not necessarily twice as beautiful as ten.

Colour nearly always needs extra consideration in anniversary flowers for any event. One may be asked to produce the patriotic colours representing a nation, memorial wreaths for a British Legion anniversary, or the racing colours of a certain jockey.

Here we are discussing golden wedding flowers, and for these the background should be as simple as possible, and in tone with the group. Remove, for the time being, anything which introduces another colour and make sure, too, that the containers and accessories are chosen to fit into the scheme.

In this photograph, the flowers stand towards one end of the mantelshelf, well out of the way, but easily seen above shoulder height.

Anyone who frequently arranges large groups will know the importance of 'filling in' material and in midsummer suitable flowers are not difficult to find. The gold group consists chiefly of stems of *Achillea* Moonshine, sprays of the evergreen *Euonymus radicans*, with branches of golden privet which provide the outline. Each is easy to grow, unfussy about soil conditions, and all the better for cutting once established. The three yellow lupins, stems of phlomis, roses, honeysuckle and sisyrinchium merely give a colour emphasis and a shading of deeper and lighter tones within the theme.

More contrast is provided by the dark green and cream of the lupin leaves and the almost blue-green of achillea stems.

In the gold group, the yellow anthemis daisy could be useful with Golden Showers or Gloire de Dijon roses, the latter adding a subtle tone of soft apricot. The pale lemon-coloured fluffy heads of *Thalictrum glaucum* on tall stems could replace the lupins and the round daisylike flowers of cephalaria would also give height. Any of the hypericums would provide a true golden yellow as would certain of the yellow irises, or there might be a yellow eremurus available.

With so many flowers and branches it is essential to have a container of the right colour which will hold plenty of water, as in hot weather the level is likely to fall some distance every day.

Special occasions come into most people's lives at one time or another. Some of them may be accompanied by specially composed

Flowers for a golden wedding anniversary – yellow lupins, deeper yellow achillea, honeysuckle, sisyrinchium, yellow roses, phlomis and branches of *Euonymus radicans* and golden privet

music; many of them may depend on ceremonial dress and procedure, but almost all of them demand decorations with flowers. Flowers can adapt themselves to any mood and any occasion.

It is interesting, too, to notice the significance that certain flowers have for certain occasions, and to discover that many of these associations are based on customs and legends, probably hundreds of years old.

In some cases the colour of a flower is almost as significant as the flower itself, and this applies especially here in the case of a silver wedding celebration. White is still considered especially suitable for a bride, although until the Middle Ages it was the colour worn for mourning. In 1498 Queen Anne, wife of Charles VIII of France, was one of the first to introduce the wearing of black for a funeral. Yellow was a colour of mourning in Egypt, while in India it is believed to bring good luck and is the colour considered to be sacred to Buddha.

Some twenty-five years ago in England a dark red carnation was considered the only possible colour and flower for a gentleman's buttonhole, and only violets might be worn with hunting pink. The origin of the buttonhole is sometimes connected with Prince Albert. The story goes that before her betrothal Queen Victoria gave a rose from her bouquet to Prince Albert, who immediately slashed a slit in the lapel of his tunic into which he fixed the flower.

The Victorians and the Edwardians used orchids and carnations to a great extent for bouquets. There is a record of a large bouquet made for Queen Alexandra composed entirely of orchids in tones of lilac and pink with sprays of maidenhair fern tied with lilac satin ribbon, and another one of the red and white carnation Marmion tied with white ribbon for the Empress of Russia. But the appreciation of flowers of more humble origin is at last showing itself in arrangements for special occasions, linked with an equal regard for different kinds of foliage.

In the white (or silver) group, the three main constituents are foxgloves, sweet rocket and *Stachys lanata*. All three, though officially white or grey, are quite different in shade, and all are simple and unsophisticated.

The foxglove colours range from deep cream in the tight buds to fully opened cream-white flowers, the *Stachys lanata* provide soft velvety dark grey leaves with lighter grey flower spikes still in bud, and sweet rocket has the pure white flowers of the soap flake advertisements – even whiter than the arums – with clear green foliage that gives a real feeling of depth.

Many other flowers could have been used in this group: white campanulas (*Campanula persicifolia alba*), white delphiniums, marguerites, ox-eye daisies, hedge parsley, or Félicité et Perpétue roses.

Most colour schemes for church decoration need careful thought, but at Easter time whatever flowers are available are gladly put to use.

Silver wedding flowers, including white foxgloves, arum lilies and sweet rocket

A group of *Narcissus* Cheerfulness with willow catkins and the fresh green leaves of flowering currant at St Paul's church, Covent Garden

Opposite: A pedestal group for Easter decoration in St Paul's church, Covent Garden, consisting of branches of forsythia with deep green laurel foliage

Forsythia and daffodils are the two arranged in our pictures at St Paul's Church, Covent Garden.

The dignity of this 17th-century Inigo Jones church, with carving by Grinling Gibbons, would be spoiled by fussy flowers. The simple lines of construction are beautiful in themselves: any floral addition must fit into this classical surrounding.

In the case of the forsythia, which is admirable for a pedestal group, the selection of a container to stand in the chancel was difficult. However, it appeared that either iron or stoneware would fit in best with the atmosphere, and the ironwork of the altar rail gave the clue. The metal pedestal, one of the simplest designs I have seen, was made by Mr R. A. R. Moseley, of The Forge, Appledore, Kent.

The white porcelain Staffordshire vase filled with double narcissi stands in a less formal position, but shows up well against the dark woodwork of the pulpit.

Now we come to the flowers themselves. The forsythia is held in position by large-mesh wire netting and by the support of large branches of evergreen laurel. The well-shaped, solid laurel leaves provide both contrast and depth of colour. Their woody stems have been crushed or split to allow greater intake of water.

One way of getting a shrub like forsythia to flower at the appropriate time is to plant two shrubs in different positions so that one of them should be ready just when needed. One of my own shrubs grows against a sheltered, south-facing wall: as its last flowers begin to drop the other, which stands in an exposed, grassy area battered by south-westerly gales, comes into bloom.

The narcissi in the white bowl are not home grown. Bought in the market, they had few leaves with them, so branches of flowering currant, pussy willow and hazel catkins were used as a background, and arranged in large-mesh wire netting. The fresh green of the currant – some of the first greenery to appear in the garden – is especially valuable.

The narcissi buds were supplemented by tight daffodil ones. It is the use of these flowers in different stages of bloom in an arrangement which helps to give the natural look of a garden-picked bunch. Especially attractive varieties are Cheerfulness and Beersheba.

Leaves and branches to go with them are not such a problem to enumerate. First among these I would place wild arum leaves; branches of rosemary; short spikes of bursting lilac foliage and *Viburnum fragrans*; the dark, fanlike leaves of *Helleborus foetidus* and some of the smaller new fresh leaves of bergenia.

I have heard the comment that daffodils and narcissi do not last well, but have seldom found this to be so. They must be fresh and the tips of the stems must be snipped off before arranging, but, given reasonable conditions, once in water they should last quite well. Like any other flowers they do not like to be exposed to varying degrees of temperature, so keep them out of draughts, away from radiators or fires and check the water level.

Spring Arrangements

When collecting material from the garden or the countryside in springtime it always surprises me to notice the various stages of buds and leaves. Because spring is almost here, it does not mean that everything is nearly or fully out. Wild arum leaves have appeared in the hedgerows and foxglove leaves in sheltered positions in the garden, but many branches of shrubs and trees are still in tight bud. The *Viburnum fragrans* and *V. bodnantense* have both been producing clustered pink blossoms for some time, but there are no leaves to speak of yet. The golden-yellow flowers of forsythia may be gladdening our hearts, and if we brought some of the knobbly brown branches indoors a month ago the flowers may have come out earlier, but the foliage is still to come.

Among the certainties are hazel catkins, hanging brown and rather curled up through the coldest weather, but now breaking out into 'thin yellow caterpillars', as Mr Andrew Young describes them in *A Prospect of Flowers*.

There are also the golden puffs along the thin stems of willow gleaming by the side of a stream or shooting up their tall spikes from a boggy meadow. So often they time their flowering conveniently for Easter and so for church decoration. And there is the splendour of horse chestnut already breaking out into exciting shoots. To bring a few branches indoors and watch these sticky buds unfolding is surely one of the most dramatic sights of spring.

In the hedgerows there may be long, slender sprays of honeysuckle bearing fresh green shoots, and in the garden there should be fat, olive-green lilac buds with their promise of later flowers and leaves. In the garden, too, there may be the bright green of flowering currant (*Ribes sanguineum*) and this always seems to me to be the time of its real value. Later on, when there are many other green leaves available, the flowering currant foliage becomes heavier in colouring and sometimes can look almost dowdy. But in early spring the freshness of the solid leaves is unequalled – they stand out among other bare branches as a beacon, defying the cold east winds. Their scent does not seem so stifling or perhaps it is less noticeable because they are so welcome.

Just as early comes the smaller and darker glistening leaves of japonica (chaenomeles). There are various colourings of this flower and one of the most delightful is the one known as apple blossom with palest pink, almost white flowers, deepening to a rosy flush.

Although most spring flowers are in the shops by this time and

A tall pedestal group of spring branches including lilac, horse chestnut, willow, forsythia and japonica

A bunch of the first snowdrops arranged in a dark green glass on a round bread-board. In front of it are violets surrounded by moss, and there are two or three woodland branches to complete this picture of early spring

some of them out in the woods or in our gardens, they are not usually available in great numbers and are still quite expensive to buy. And so this is the month for small groups of violets or snow-drops, grape hyacinths or anemones, primroses or scillas, either arranged in separate bunches or grouped to give a 'tussie-mussie' effect – that is, a few of each put together to make up an attractive spring nosegay.

Any such small arrangements take on a new significance in the evening if they stand in the light of a reading lamp, each flower glowing in its bright and cheerful colouring.

Small arrangements require small containers and so it is wise to put away any vases which hold quantities of flowers and bring out some of those which are only capable of holding a few. Woodland flowers such as violets, snowdrops, primroses or wood anemones seem to look happiest when arranged in damp moss so that they appear to be still growing naturally. Here in this photograph the snowdrops are in a small glass jar supported in its position by the moss. The moss is lying amongst the twigs and flowers on a round wooden breadboard, and is kept damp by a daily shower from a small flower spray. The water supply of the flowers must be carefully watched, especially in the case of the violets, and kept topped up regularly.

I would like to point out that the moss in this group will not cause dampness if it is only sprayed, and that the darker colouring on the breadboard is the natural marking. Its rather rough texture is suitable to the woodland flowers, the moss and the small branches.

Although this is a small arrangement, it may be noticed that the foliage of the flowers plays a not insignificant part in the general design. The leaves of the snowdrops are an essential factor in producing a natural effect and the very beautiful violet leaves are dramatic in outline and a good Robin Hood green in colour, a perfect foil to the delicate flowers.

Snowdrops are in most gardens and are so well known and loved that they are likely to be the first flowers of the year for many households. A small bunch brought indoors are a joy, and they will last quite well (contrary, I think, to general belief). Sometimes inexplicably, as with a bunch of primroses, one or two of the flowers will die off before the others and if these are taken out the others will continue to flourish. But left in they immediately give their tired look to the whole vase, and I have sometimes seen all the contents of such a vase thrown out when there was still life in most of the other flowers. When they are first coming in snowdrops are especially precious and should, it seems to me, be guarded like gold.

It is not always realized that there are many different kinds of snowdrop, one of which was brought from the Crimea by a Captain Aldington during the Crimean War. The R.H.S. gardens at Wisley have a fine collection, many of which have come from the gardens of the late Sir Frederick Stern.

Hellebores are amongst the first spring flowers to give us delight in the garden. The pale green flowers and darker green leaves of *Helleborus foetidus* contrast with the red anemones

In this small arrangement a few red anemones are contrasted with the dark, slender leaves of *Helleborus foetidus* and the pale green clusters of its flowers. Sprays of variegated periwinkle and the dead nettle, *Lamium galeobdolon variegatum*, help to carry on the gentle curves of the sauceboat into quite a spreading group which might be suitable perhaps for a narrow dining table or a windowsill position.

Other leaves available for use with spring flowers include wild arum leaves, berberis in fresh green shoots, laurustinus, flowering currant, budding viburnum, pussy willow and hazel catkins, alder catkins, larch, silver shoots of whitebeam, bergenia, Corsican hellebore, Lenten hellebore and the dark fanlike clusters of pieris foliage. Purple-sprouting broccoli and the rather knobbly, brown branches of sea buckthorn (hippophae) before it comes into leaf make an interesting contrast.

In the hope that new and exciting ideas may be tried, a variety of plants are included amongst these suggestions for growing in the garden to provide leaves which are especially suitable for indoor decoration.

For a large garden of, say, over half an acre, this list may not be comprehensive enough. It may, on the other hand, be too ambitious for a very small town garden, which might be handicapped by the poor quality of the soil, or its aspect, or the mere incapacity to accommodate so much material. It is one thing to make out, optimistically, a list of things to grow and quite another to find a comfortable place for each of them – a place where each will be growing under the right conditions. Indiscriminate planting without careful planning beforehand, quite apart from being unfair to the plants themselves, can also be a complete waste of time and money.

There is no doubt that attractive and long-lasting foliage is one of the most useful assets of a garden and an absolute necessity if one has to be economical. But the use of foliage seems to depend very much on the appreciation of green as a colour, the different tones and shades which are possible within that colour, and on the importance of design in the structure and habit of growth of individual species.

In almost any book on Japanese flower work, space is devoted to illustrations of camellia leaves, bamboo canes, and branches of maple, cedar, pine and willow. This has only recently happened in English books on the same subject.

Perhaps here lies the secret. Respect for green growing things is not a new idea; rather it is something we have lost sight of and which we should do well to recover. In our zeal for art and originality we may be inclined to overlook the truth and beauty of natural things. 'The greatest and the fairest things are done by nature and the lesser by Art' (Plato). Sometimes it seems as though ordinary observance is dulled and blunted and only something outstanding in colour or shape or size qualifies for notice. And all the time there are the soft shades and beautiful shapes, deep tones and architectural structures of leaf to be seen and appreciated and used.

It is interesting and rewarding to experiment in arousing this perception by looking at something we may take for granted with a completely new approach, such as, for instance, a rosette of London pride, or a spray of ivy-leaved toadflax growing on a cottage wall; to examine carefully a clump of velvet moss, or a stem of clear-pointed, dark, shining ivy. These plants often live their lives through with little recognition, because we are so accustomed to them and to seeing them in their natural setting. Jason Hill writes: 'We know so surely that the clump of fennel will reappear where it was planted, that the sculptural beauty of its sea-green columnar stems and the moulding of its pale bracts usually develop and pass unnoticed.'

And so the two most important factors in the use of foliage seem to be firstly the development of line arrangements, and secondly the contrasts possible between the different shapes and textures and colours of leaves. In the latter case it is as though one type of leaf takes the place of the flower in the group, and the other acts as a background or as a setting for it by virtue of its distinctive shape or colour. The development of line in connection with branches is obvious, and beautiful and striking silhouette effects can be obtained.

It should be remembered that most foliage likes a large amount of water to drink but if the container is kept filled to the brim, time and patience will be well repaid.

Arranged opposite in the white porcelain jelly mould are four firm favourites of spring. The sparkling blue of forget-me-nots, the glowing colours and sweet scent of wallflowers, the grace and charm of pale lilac spires of milkmaids (or lady's smock or cuckoo flower) and the much-loved gentle velvets of auriculas – without growing any other springtime flowers a brave show could be made with these alone.

There is no need to extol either of the first two for the garden, although the full value of forget-me-nots for flower arrangement sometimes seems to be unappreciated. Perhaps they are rather untidy to cut, sometimes may even to the meticulously minded appear to be sprawling, but how worth while they prove to be, each small flower and bud perfect in its shape and colouring. Forget-me-nots last quite well and will go on coming out in water in succession if the first flowers to die are cut off as soon as they begin to wither.

Wallflowers, cut quite short here to form a framework for the smaller flowers, provide rich colourings as well as a sweet scent. Sometimes it pays to cut them short from the point of view of lasting, as this also automatically reduces the number of leaves on the stem which take up quite a quantity of water.

Now we come to lady's smock. Generally thought of as a wild plant, this most charming, delicately coloured flower will usually colonize happily in a damp patch of ground in the garden or in a border of long grass. A small bunch of these flowers can, to my mind, bring into the house a real feeling that spring has come. Unlike some wild flowers planted in the garden they do not multiply to the extent of getting quickly out of control. The small, darkish, rather thin clumps of leaves are distinguishable even before the plant sends up its tall, thin flower stem, and these are quite easy to dig up if there are too many of them. My chief concern is to get them to establish themselves energetically enough. I have them growing close by a narrow watercourse and am delighted to see that they seem to be at home there. A small bunch standing in a wineglass makes a charming decoration.

Perhaps my favourite of all early flowering plants is the auricula. In order to protect them from the onslaught of slugs and snails and other greedy pests I have them in select seclusion in a large old bucket which has a few small bits of stone in it to make them feel at home. They do well in these circumstances and perhaps soon I may gain enough courage to plant them out to stand up to the general stresses and strains of the garden.

I have mentioned already that the container for these flowers is a white porcelain jelly mould given to me by my stepdaughter with the firm injunction that it was not to be used for cooking but *only* for flowers. I should never have thought of using a jelly mould for this purpose, and am grateful for her suggestion. It has proved ideal, especially for short-stemmed flowers.

As forget-me-nots feature in this flower group, I should like to mention an idea for planting them which originated from one of the large gardens open to the public. There was a photograph of one of these gardens showing a wide sweep of grass going out of picture in a deep curve. Bordering the grass was a sowing of forget-me-nots, and behind them an evergreen hedge of some dimensions. The final effect was as though a strip of bright blue sky had been brought down to earth to encircle this patch of green. Immediately one longed, as with a rainbow, to discover where it touched the ground, entirely because the blue ribbon of forget-me-nots disappeared out of sight round the corner.

Ordinarily it might be felt that the dimensions were too enormous to try out such an idea in a small garden, but all that was needed was, in fact, a curve of grass and a sowing of forget-me-nots (it was possible to dispense with the hedge). I tried it out in my own country garden, and for three years running it became one of the focal points of my planting. Visitors said to me: 'What a lovely line of blue – it looks almost as though the sky is reflected in a strip of water.' The whole point of the plan hinged on the simple fact that the curve went just out of sight round the corner, inviting one to follow.

As Miss Jekyll wrote in *Wood and Garden* about the coming of distant summer early in the year when 'the day always comes and with it the glad certainty that summer is nearing and that the good things promised will never fail', so there are usually a few false alarms about spring. There may be separate days when one is tempted to believe that it has actually arrived and then down comes the snow and fiercely blows the east wind and we turn thankfully again to the comfort of our central heating. But with the coming of the daffodils we can take heart and feel that spring has come at last.

The arrival of spring can mean different things for different people

Forget-me nots, auriculas, milkmaids (cardamine) and wallflowers are clustered together in a white porcelain jelly mould

Primroses are arranged here with many of their leaves and buds in a small cream porcelain basket

in various parts of the country. By the side of Rydal Water the daffodils announce its arrival, while in south Cornwall the blue clusters of squills on the rocky shore or the bright green leaves of alexanders along the hedgerow are both evidence of its coming. For Miles Hadfield it was on hearing the chiff-chaff for the first time that 'one knows that the full power of spring's unleashed'. Anyone who has seen the damson blossom dappling the bare hills with fairy white in North Lancashire will know the feeling of spring which this particular sight can give.

In our county of Kent we find that the time of the blossom varies greatly from one year to another. Sometimes the cherry blossom is out in time for decorating the church at Easter, depending not only on whether Easter is early or late but on the blossom itself; sometimes it is not fully out until much later and something else must be found for church decoration.

Just as daffodils and narcissi are happily associated with trees of blossom standing in meadow grass, so they seem to associate well with branches for indoor decoration. It would be difficult to have to decide which is the most lovely of all the fruit blossoms – the purity of the white cherry or pear, the friendliness of a rosy-tinted apple flower or the simplicity of the larger-petalled quince. The cherry in the photograph on pages 62–63 with its pale leaves tinged with brown makes a delightful framework for the more sturdy-looking daffodils and straight-stemmed narcissi arranged with it.

The lasting qualities of any of the fruit blossoms are surprisingly good especially if they are cut when still in bud and the base of each branch is split open or crushed to allow for a greater intake of water. The daffodils only need the ends of their stems snipping off, if they have not been cut straight from the garden. This gets rid of the small gluey area of sap which accumulates to prevent it running out but also effectively stops the water entering up the stalk.

Where to begin in mentioning specific daffodils or narcissi? This is already a large family which is being developed every year. There are 400 varieties of narcissus grown in the Scilly Isles alone and each farm grows 30 to 50 of these varieties. Based on my own experience or on expert recommendation I will mention certain varieties in various groups which are especially good for cutting.

The first to come out – a special favourite for that reason and also on account of their perfect proportions in such a small daffodil – are the wild Welsh Lent lilies (*Narcissus pseudonarcissus*). These are in full flower in early spring and their first buds are in evidence at least a week before. When ordering these from a nurseryman I encountered more difficulty and cost in obtaining them than any others that I needed.

Other favourite varieties are Pheasant's Eye, Angel's Tears, Cheerfulness and Beersheba. The true poet's narcissus (*N. poeticus*) is also lovely, and a new variety is recommended, named Shanach. Another, a dwarf one, *N. poeticus radiiflorus,* is late-flowering, as late as mid-June. Mrs O. Backhouse, with a perianth of ivory white and a slim trumpet of apricot and almost shell pink at the edge, is now well known. Mitylene also has a large white perianth with a wide, shallow cup of almost primrose yellow. A fine white daffodil is *Narcissus* Empress of Ireland, and ice white with green at the base of its perfectly balanced trumpet is Castle of Mey. *Narcissus* Victory has a large scarlet cup against broad yellow petals. A white flower which earns high praise for the garden and for cutting is Cantatrice, which has won leading prizes all over the world. The whole flower is pure white.

There are so many to choose from, and a good way to see them is to go to a spring flower show such as the Royal Horticultural Society Spring Show and make a selection.

There are also many gardens open to the public where there are carpets of spring bulbs and daffodils. This is especially so at Wisley and Kew. Probably one of the most wonderful sights of springtime is to be seen in the Savill Gardens at Windsor. The daffodil plantings – there are tens of thousands of them – are on grassy slopes under the bare branches of oak and the new foliage of beech and silver birch, and bordering grass paths.

Both daffodils and polyanthuses are sometimes criticized on the grounds that they do not always last well in water. In the case of daffodils this may have some basis of truth if the flowers are not absolutely fresh when cut for arrangement.

It may also be helpful to give them a deep drink in a bucket of water first (they like to drink through the walls of their stems as well

A basket of cherry blossom and narcissi

as up them) even if they are cut and brought straight in from the garden or bought while still fresh from a reliable florist.

When arranged they appreciate standing out of a draught, away from any excessive form of heating. More than anything, they dislike a draught and because we sometimes see a vase of drooping narcissi or polyanthuses standing on a ledge over a central heating radiator under an open window (this sometimes happens in a hospital ward) we may be inclined to criticize all spring flowers.

To prove my argument I once, at Easter time, arranged narcissi on a grave in a country churchyard, in an exposed position, where they lasted well for nearly a fortnight.

Polyanthuses react in much the same way, certainly to draughts which they also very much dislike. But planted out in the garden – if you can keep the birds away – they will produce most magnificent patches of colour. Brilliant sometimes, deep and penetrating or pale and clear, they come in some variety and with a sweet woodland scent.

I am inclined to think of them growing more effectively in a town garden than almost anywhere else and hope that country gardeners will forgive my saying so. We all know and appreciate the beauty of town parks and public gardens, but sometimes it is the smaller and more unexpected bits of planting which catch at the heart. For example, one of the sights of the City of London in springtime is, to my mind, the square bed of polyanthuses set like jewels of topaz and garnet in an area of grass across the road from St Paul's Cathedral. The bed is only a few feet wide but the impact is quite astonishing.

This same kind of effect can be achieved by a small bunch for the house.

In the photograph opposite they are clustered together into a large breakfast cup and saucer. Some anchorage may be helpful as the inside of the cup is slippery and this could be supplied either by crumpled-up Oasis or wire netting. The polyanthus stems are not usually firm enough to penetrate into solid Oasis and will probably break if put to the test.

One of the difficulties in arranging polyanthuses may be the weight of the flowers bearing down the cluster of slender stems before they join the main central stem. This can give an effect of flopping unless the flower heads are supported which must be done in as natural a way as possible. The rim of the cup provides the support in this case as the flowers can rest against it, the main stems being cut quite short. As with most flowers growing in clusters, their life may be prolonged by cutting off any dead ones and allowing the buds to come out in their turn.

Tolerance is an endearing characteristic, shining through the many problems of everyday life. A good argument can be invigorating and clear the air, but it is the courtesy of tolerance which helps to smooth out the most prickly situations. There are many subjects that can be expected to be controversial, when one has only to mention a

Brightly coloured polyanthuses
in a cup-and-saucer arrangement

preference to become aware of the great differences of opinion. But somehow with flowers it is surprising to come up against deeply felt opposition to certain ideas.

It seems that there is a school of thought which does not approve of using mixed flowers, or even two different kinds of flowers, in one arrangement.

There seems to me to be no reason why the same kind of flowers should not be arranged separately or, again, should not be mixed with quite different ones. The idea that this should not be so has, I must confess, come to my notice only within the last few years.

However, most viewpoints and ideas are interesting and worthy of being explored, and it may be a good thing that they should at least be aired and given a chance to survive. Though a mixed bunch of flowers from an English garden has always seemed to me one of the most expressive forms of indoor decoration in this country, I must be tolerant of the idea that to some people this is not permissible.

But at least I have stated the case and I am illustrating it by the use of the polyanthuses in the photograph.

Some of the most welcome and delightful flower groups are surely those which are brought in from the garden in early spring. I am thinking of the first snowdrops with a few winter aconites, two or three stems of lilac-blue *Iris stylosa* and a spray of *Viburnum fragrans*. According to the idea of using only one kind of flower, such an arrangement would not be possible.

Bright pink anemones with grape
hyacinths, bergenia flowers, heather and
rosemary

I hope my effort to illustrate this point will be taken as it is meant,
an honest attempt to stake a claim for something which is regarded
seriously by some flower arrangers. My own ideas about a mixed
garden bunch do not by any means eliminate the use of one kind of
flower at a time. For instance, on certain occasions I have used arum
lilies (and admired greatly such a group in Canterbury cathedral),
roses, bluebells, buttercups, gentians and carnations, all arranged
without other flowers.

This photograph illustrates a typical garden bunch for late spring
in a variety of colours.

With the exception of a few anemones, all the flowers – primroses,
bergenia, rosemary, grape hyacinths, heathers – are small and cut
with short stems. The anemones, all selected in the same tone from
one bunch, provide the dominant colour. A different effect could be
achieved by using purple-blue ones, or even red, when the pink
bergenia might perhaps be excluded.

Again, a yellow scheme could include small wild daffodils but no
anemones; the other flowers could be the same, the soft blue of the
grape hyacinths making an interesting contrast with the clear yellow
of the daffodils. Sprays of rosemary may provide a light touch of

grey-green, with anemone fronds and primrose leaves to give an
extra depth of green and variety of shape.

As it is the rosemary which provides a framework for this group I
should, perhaps, give a few cultural comments on this favourite and
useful shrub.

Rosmarinus officinalis, a hardy or half-hardy evergreen shrub, will
flourish in ordinary soil but it likes a dryish, sunny position.
Everyone knows – and probably loves – the charming, scented foliage
of this plant. Cuttings may easily be taken from rosemary in
September, put into sand and allowed to grow on until the next
spring when they should be ready to plant out.

The common rosemary, *R. officinalis*, is splendid for cutting as it
sends out many upright shoots as well as being sturdy itself. These
upright shoots make useful additions to foliage arrangements not only
on account of their colour and the shape of the leaves but because
they can be depended on to keep straight and firm. A rosemary that I
love is *R. officinalis angustifolius* Corsicus. It has a much lighter type
of leaf, almost feathery, and is altogether a more delicate-looking
plant than the species, *R. officinalis*. The colour of the flower is a
wonderful deep blue.

A small white porcelain double basket, a Victorian ornament, has been used here for a simple arrangement. *Narcissus* Paper White and Soleil d'Or and white freesias have been cut short to keep them in proportion to the container. The small stems of foliage are pittosporum

Narcissi and freesias are both flowers with almost bare stems, and as we have been discussing rosemary used with anemones and grape hyacinths, this may be a good moment to talk about pittosporum which is used here. These are only short sprays – it comes in tall branches – but they are enough to furnish the small vase with leaves. Their pale colouring is good with the narcissi and cream-white freesias.

A half-hardy flowering shrub, the pittosporum likes to grow in a fibrous peat, loam and silver sand, usually in a fairly sheltered position. In gardens north of London one is even advised to bring it into a cool greenhouse for the winter. It may be planted in the spring and propagation is by cuttings of moderately firm shoots inserted in sandy soil under glass.

This is a florist's shrub, usually appearing in bunches in the shops throughout the winter and in the early spring when other foliage may be difficult to find, in company with grevillea and eucalyptus. It is

used as a windbreak round the bulb fields in the Isles of Scilly, and two of the species, *P. crassifolium* and *P. ralphii* are described as being 'most wind-hardy, rapid and erect-growing'. Unfortunately they are not frost hardy. The former is reported to have survived severe gales in the Western Isles, but is expected to succumb if faced by an acute frost. *P. tenuifolium* has survived for many years in the South West of England, especially in Cornwall and Devon. It is also grown to a great extent in Somerset for marketing purposes.

Other pittosporums are *P. bicolor*, with narrow leaves at first white-felted and later brown-felted below, and small brown and yellow flowers; *P. buchananii*, with thin leaves and purple flowers sometimes growing to a height of 15 ft in suitable surroundings; and *P. undulatum*, which has handsome, fragrant, creamy-white flowers and has been known to achieve a height of nearly 30 ft. For cutting it is completely reliable, but should be used with discretion owing to its rather fussy outline.

Just as it is impossible to disassociate Wordsworth from daffodils, so, I imagine, it is also difficult to think of blossom without Herrick: 'Fair pledges of a fruitful tree, Why do ye fall so fast?' and 'What! were ye born to be an hour or half's delight, and so to bid goodnight?' In fact, if one can only indulge in a few trees of different kinds one might first see the damson trees as in the Lyth Valley, then the cherry and pear trees as in Kent, and a fortnight or so later, one may watch the miracle of opening apple buds in any of the fruit-growing counties.

But, in spite of poetic licence, was Herrick right about blossom if it is cut for arrangements in the house?

My own experience has been that if it is cut early enough, while still in bud when it usually looks at its most engaging, it will come out and oblige with the same good behaviour as wild flowers or any other blossom which is reputed not to last long, that is, quite long enough for it to be possible to have enjoyed it and to have seen at close hand the beauty of the unfolding buds and wide-opened flowers.

And then, again, comes the argument, should one really cut branches from a tree for the sake of the flower which, later on in the year, would produce apples, pears, or plums? Well, this may be a case for one's own conscience. But I have seen so many apples lying rotting in the long orchard grass, plums eaten by wasps, cherries providing an excellent dinner for the tits, sparrows, starlings and bullfinches that I cannot feel any compunction about taking a branch or two for the decoration of a house where the appreciation may be more visual than culinary but none the less for that. It is possible, perhaps – using sharp secateurs and choosing branches which will not harm the shape of the tree – even to do some useful pruning.

I have sometimes heard gardeners complain about a tree that bears plenty of blossom but not much fruit. This may be a tragedy to a commercial fruit grower, but in a garden surely the beauty of the blossom counts for something and should be appreciated for its own sake.

The Japanese regard blossom with the respect and appreciation that it deserves. The month of April – the third month of the old spring, as they call it – is the month of the cherry blossom and at this time branches of cherry, plum and peach are the usual materials for flower arrangements.

Excursions are made to see the blossom in flower, as they are in certain areas of this country, and arrangements are composed of branches with the buds and flowers when they are in different stages of development. Sometimes it is felt that a half-opened flower is more powerful than a fully opened one, and so a branch which is still in bud may be used as a main stem in a group with surrounding branches of flowers which are almost out. Varieties which flower later (there is, for instance, a summer-flowering peach grown in Japan) may not be used as this would be regarded as unnatural.

Since the Japanese try to arrange their material as far as possible

A few branches of apple blossom
arranged in a brown earthenware dish to
show their outline

as it would be if it were still growing, fruit branches are not crowded
in among other flowers but are allowed to be seen as individual
shapes. 'Whereas the Western amateur devotes his attention mainly
to the blossoms, the Japanese lover of flowers bestows his admiration
on the whole character of the plant or tree producing them . . . The
lines of branch and stem, the form and surfaces of leaves, and the
distribution of buds and blossoms, all receive their full share of
attention. The loveliest buds and blossoms torn from their stems and
crushed together in a mass with ferns or other greenery between
them, convey to the Japanese mind no idea of floral art or beauty.'

There is no reason to follow Japanese ideas in most of our floral
decorations but it seems to me that this particular point is worthy of
adoption. The shape of the branch, the position of the leaves, the
half-opened buds – these are all parts of a composite picture just as
much as the fully opened flowers.

An arrangement of this kind should stand against a plain background so that the outline of the group can be seen clearly as well as
the detail of the blossom.

The appreciation of foliage seems to depend largely on the value of green as a colour with the different tones and shades ranging from pale lime green or a soft grey-green to the darkest camellia or holly leaf which may sometimes almost appear to be black.

The opening lines of many verses in Chinese poetry have the words 'Green, green . . .':
'Green, green, those elm-tree leaves . . .'
'Green, green, the grass by the river bank . . .'
'Green, green, the cypress on the mound . . .'
With the possible exceptions of Arthur Hugh Clough and Andrew Marvell, not many English poets seem to write about this insistence on green as a colour, which is reflected again in the Eastern feeling for foliage generally and especially with reference to arrangement for indoor decoration. Writing at the turn of the century, the garden designer William Robinson remarks on the importance of form and line learnt from the Japanese.

It is really a question of appreciating the value of line and subtlety of tone and detail rather than craving for the blaze of colour beloved of the seed packets. Jason Hill in *The Contemplative Gardener* suggested that 'it is doubtful if we like mere brightness in flowers any better than we do in people,' and then goes on '. . . there is a great deal of beauty . . . if only we do not insist upon flowers and if we are willing to regard green and brown as colours.'

This appreciation of outline in foliage or respect for green growing things is not a new idea. The architecture of Southwell and many of its stone carvings depend on the contrast of an ivy leaf or maple, oak, vine, hawthorn and hop. The wood carvings of Grinling Gibbons certainly included flowers, but these were well supplied with foliage as an accompaniment. Durer found excitement and interest in a small patch of turf resulting in a painting full of tender detail and love for the small things of nature, and with not a flower to be seen.

And what about the addition of white with green? The small green-and-white-tipped flowers of Solomon's seal immediately introduce the idea and demonstrate in one plant how attractive the two colours can be.

This is a plant which grows well in almost any kind of soil although it may prefer leafmould. It should be planted in a partially shaded position, or under trees, either in the autumn or spring, when an annual topdressing of farmyard manure may be helpful.

Polygonatum multiflorum (David's harp) grows to a height of about 3 ft and flowers during late spring. It is essentially a plant for the semi-wild part of the garden. If flower beds are trim and neat with no patches of long grass or bits of woodland, it may be difficult to find a suitable planting place for it.

The charm of Solomon's seal for cutting is evident. The curving

The shape of the leaves and delicate green and white flowers of Solomon's seal are shown off in this simple glass jar

sprays of beautifully shaped, clear green leaves arranged in pairs are a gift in themselves apart from the contrast of the green and white flowers. They last well and, even when the flowers are over, the foliage is still available to give a graceful line and shape to a large arrangement.

Discussing further the use of foliage and green material, it seems that the two most important factors are the development of line arrangements, and the contrasts possible between the different shapes and textures and colours of leaves. In the latter case it is as though one type of leaf takes the place of the flower in the group and the other acts as a setting for it by virtue of its distinctive shape and colour, and an example is shown of this in the photograph. The rounded – although serrated – shape and colouring of the cranesbill contrasts with the curving shape and fresh, variegated colouring of the *Hosta undulata* and the thin, bright-coloured leaves of the pieris. An arrangement using this type of material not only has the advantage of looking cool during the first hot days of late spring weather, but will also last literally for two or three weeks if required to do so, as long as it is kept well supplied with water. It is a group of plants which can be available in the garden for cutting purposes from late spring until early autumn.

Some ideas for contrasts in tones of green and shapes of foliage come in the following suggestions:

1. Branches of silver-grey-green buckthorn with two or three giant deep green horseradish leaves.
2. Branches of cotoneaster with the flat, oval leaves of laurel.
3. Spreading branches of escallonia interlaced with bold stems of a large-leaved ivy.
4. The distinctive grey-green foliage of the globe artichoke with spearlike iris or gladiolus leaves or rounded bergenia leaves.
5. Thin branches of broom contrasting with long, curving sprays of summer jasmine.
6. Golden privet with holly.
7. Variegated periwinkle with dark green camellia foliage.
8. Hart's tongue fern with small-leaved ivy.
9. *Senecio laxifolius* (garden ragwort), lungwort and tufts of fennel with dark tree-peony leaves.

As so many of the ideas one uses for indoor decoration come originally from a garden – either a special bit of planting where one leaf contrasts with another or one tree looks well against another (for example, I am thinking of a guelder rose coming into flower beside the dark rich purple-brown of a prunus in a garden near our village) – perhaps it may be of interest to quote from an article published some years ago in a daily newspaper on the well-known National Trust garden of Hidcote Manor, Gloucestershire, which bears on this matter of brown and green and colours. Mr Harry Burrows, the head gardener, describes the chief point of this garden: 'But always wherever you go – colour. That's the aim. Colour all the year round.

Hosta and pieris foliage with cranesbill in a white cornucopia

It doesn't necessarily have to come from flowers. People don't always realize the wonderful colour effects that can be achieved with different shades of green, with the bark of trees, with combinations of stone, even with reflections on the water . . . But, of course, talk of colour and it is flowers that most people think of.' (Extract from *Daily Mail*, 7 May 1966.)

In late spring there are certain leaves which may not be completely dependable when they first come out. Some leaves, in spite of looking sturdy enough, are still tender and if needed for arrangement may not be tough enough to stand firmly as required, unless they are first given a good soak. Sometimes it is even helpful to lay them in a shallow bath before using them, so that they can drink their fill. Globe artichoke foliage may droop easily, as also may lungwort, lupin, foxglove and the heavy lower stems of Queen Anne's lace. Acanthus foliage is often unreliable, and certainly more so when it is first coming out.

The selection of grey-foliaged plants is now so large and varied that it is possible to plant a sizeable grey border with differences in texture, shape and shades of silver or grey which will be full of interest. Some of these plants will be dealt with later, and in the autumn there will be found further references to foliage, either with flowers or used in contrast to leaf. An autumn selection of branches and leaves seems even more extensive than that to be found in late spring.

Although it is difficult to decide on the dividing line between late spring and early summer a decision must be made and I have ended the spring chapter with a photograph which, perhaps, shows as well as anything the continuity of some flowers through various months, forming a link between two or even three seasons. Also the flowering times of plants and shrubs vary so much through the British Isles that it seems impossible to tabulate them correctly in a general way. My own experience includes a visit to Guernsey during the second week in October, where I found flowers in bloom which had finished some weeks before in England; among them cornflowers, feverfew, foxgloves, myrtle and godetia. Again, a friend tells me that she welcomed the spring three times in one year – first in the Scilly Isles, three weeks later in Berkshire, and later again in North Wales.

The material in this simple cup-and-saucer arrangement consists of narcissi, primroses, rosemary, and broom.

Narcissus comes from a large family which – thought of together – have a long flowering season. New additions are always being made, more and more varieties come on to the market, different coloured perianths appear with outside petals of another shade or size, and still they come. From the first little wild daffodils – small, delicate, in perfect proportion and with slender blue-green leaves – until the much later Pheasant's Eye and Cheerfulness is usually a period of about four months.

But if narcissi have a long flowering season, what about primroses? Sometimes one can find a clump in flower in a sheltered woodland bank in mid-autumn and on the slopes of a sunny ditch or at the foot of a sturdy thorn hedge primroses may continue to flower almost throughout the winter. But their main flowering time is the spring and they, like the narcissi, will go on right until and through tulip time. Like the narcissi, they will also last well if they are kept in a cool situation with their stems either in water or wet moss.

Rosemary was mentioned earlier in this chapter (see page 67) and has the distinction of lasting almost throughout the year. This is because it is not strictly always the flower which is cut for decoration – the foliage is practical and decorative in itself. Anyone who grows rosemary will know that this is one of the most valuable shrubs to have in the garden, not only for cutting for the house but also for its charms as a plant and the sweet scent of its leaves.

The last of these flowers in the cup and saucer is broom (cytisus), and this brings us more into line with summer-flowering shrubs. As the broom sometimes found growing wild in fir plantations is valuable for line arrangements during most months of the year, lasting well

Using a simple cup and saucer, primroses
and narcissi are arranged here with
rosemary and broom

when cut, it is often worth while having a shrub in the garden in
case one needs this kind of material.

One of the chief assets of both cytisus and genista is the shape and
type of green branch which gives an interesting outline effect, whether
the shrub is in flower or not. Some of the flowers are most decorative,
but may drop rather too quickly to be of great value for cutting.
Those of genista are usually yellow, while the cytisus, although often
yellow, can come in other colours. For our purposes I like to call
them all 'brooms'.

There are half-hardy brooms but there are many that are hardy,
both deciduous and evergreen. Most of them like light, sandy soil in
a sunny position, perhaps on a bank or in a rock garden. The hardy
brooms should be pruned directly after flowering and are best
transplanted when they are young. They are easily raised from seed.
One that is highly recommended is *Cytisus battandieri* which is
covered with yellow flowers in early summer. It also has a sweet
scent, like so many of the brooms. Then there is *Genista aethnensis*,
the Mount Etna broom, which is transformed about a month later
into a shimmering fountain.

None of the brooms cares for being disturbed once they are in
position and so when ordering a plant rather than sowing seed it may
be advisable to choose a container-grown plant which can be
planted with the least disturbance to its roots.

Summer Arrangements

Sometimes, in midsummer, there is so much profusion in the garden that it is difficult to make a selection of flowers for the house. This may be a pleasant difficulty but it is a difficulty all the same, and here again a garden can be a guide to flower arrangement. Ideas carried out in the contrast or combination of colours in a border or in the juxtaposition of planting can often provide suggestions for using those colours or plants in the same way when they are cut for indoor decoration.

The glass vase used for this arrangement has rather a shallow flat top, so a layer of Oasis, about 1 in (2 cm) deep, was cut to fit into it and this was then held in position by three squashed layers of large-mesh wire netting, the top being raised to support the taller stems. A pinholder placed in the centre of the wire netting might have done just as well, although the hosta leaves, being soft, would not anchor so happily in one.

The crisp, gaily coloured clusters of pieris would fit into any kind of anchorage but the euphorbia stems might prove to be too thin for a pinholder, so the Oasis combined with wire netting seems most suitable. The pleated leaf of *Alchemilla mollis* placed near the centre of the group provides a good contrast of plain green.

The bright new leaves of pieris are always dramatic, whether seen growing on the shrub or cut for indoor decoration. It is a most rewarding shrub to plant, giving of its bounty of colour when it is still small and newly established.

One of the finest specimens in the country is to be seen in its full glory at this time of year in the garden of Nymans, Sussex. This is the home of the Countess of Rosse and a National Trust property situated one mile from the village of Handcross, on the B2114, just off the main London to Brighton road. There are other fine examples of this shrub in the Savill Gardens, Windsor Great Park and at Wisley.

Hosta leaves are most valuable for decoration, as flower arrangers are well aware, and the one great safety measure in growing them seems to be to give the young shoots protection from slugs. Euphor-bias are legion, and sometimes I think that the wild one found in woodlands is perhaps the prettiest of all. For the garden *Euphorbia robbiae* is especially attractive with its dark rosettes of evergreen leaves providing a base for thin-stemmed paler green flower clusters.

Sprays of pieris, hosta and euphorbia in a tall glass with a pleated alchemilla leaf towards the centre

For a definite colour effect in a large arrangement, there is nothing like the long curving branches of a flowering shrub. The result is best achieved when the flowers are small and grow along the stem, so that the colour is carried all down the branch with no break in continuity.

Some of the best shrubs for cutting, flowering along the branch to the tips of their stems, are escallonia, shown in our photograph; *Spiraea argutea*, often called bridal wreath, with long, wire-thin branches which, when all the small, white flowers are out, look almost like water cascading over rocks; *Ceanothus dentatus*, evergreen, with small, dark leaves and masses of rather deep blue flowers in May; some of the genistas (brooms) and, of course, forsythia.

These are a few of the best examples although others which almost qualify are some of the azaleas, philadelphuses, weigelas, flowering currants, japonicas and the shrub briar, *Rosa hugonis*. But it is worth remembering the following points:

1. The shrub must be of a reasonable age and growth before it is cut to any extent, and should be allowed to spread so that long branches can be cut without spoiling its shape. I have found that this kind of cutting sometimes takes the place of pruning and often ensures a good display for the following season.

2. Woody stems must either be smashed at their tips or split up with strong secateurs.

3. The branches should be arranged in a container capable of holding a large supply of water.

4. The branches should be cut when not fully out so that the buds will come into flower after being arranged. Flowering shrubs are often accused of dropping quickly, but this is not usually so if they are cut early enough or purchased from a florist when the flowers are only in bud.

When grown in the garden, flowering shrubs may be incorporated in many kinds of planting and do not necessarily have to stand alone or, for that matter, in a bed kept especially for shrubs. For instance, most of them will grow happily against a wall or fence, some may be planted in a border with herbaceous plants and many make interesting material for a hedge, as well as providing a good supply of cutting material for indoor arrangements.

Pink is a colour sometimes associated with delicate or even insipid effects – like sugar candy, lollipops, cosmetics and bath salts – but pink can also be bright and dominant, capable of achieving a contrast and of holding its own in a strong furnishing colour scheme.

The escallonia in our photograph is deep enough in tone to stand up against the depth of blue in the background. It is arranged in a tall pewter urn, the stems held in position by large-mesh wire netting

Tall branches of escallonia in a pedestal arrangement. The rich pink flowers contrast with the background

81

Flowers from a cottage garden – a group
of Canterbury bells in various colours

crumpled up into three layers. The urn stands on a pedestal, ensuring
that the long, sweeping branches are seen to advantage.

So often when wandering round gardens which are open to the
public, either through the National Trust or for various charities,
one comes across a bit of planting which arrests the attention.

I myself have found certain ideas emerging from gardens of this
kind which provided the basis for many flower arrangements – not
just the one which comes to mind immediately. I have seen, for
instance, in at least two or three gardens a white flower planted close
to dark, evergreen leaves. In one case there was a planting of the
white form of *Cyclamen neapolitanum* under a walnut tree and this
in turn was interplanted with green-leaved forms of ivy against which
the white flowers showed up before their own leaves put in an
appearance. In another garden a white rose, *Rosa moschata alba*, was
climbing up and over a well-grown dark green holly. The white
cascade through the dark leaves almost gave an impression of a
waterfall. Then again there was the white rose, *Rosa filipes*, clam-
bering through the dark branches of a well-established oak, and
flaunting long white streamers through the thick foliage.

All these varied plantings in different gardens lead to the same idea,
that of using white with dark green. For flower arrangement this
may be interpreted in many ways – snowdrops with ivy leaves,

82

candidum lilies with camellia foliage, Iceberg roses with the shining green oval leaves of laurel, white delphiniums with branches of the evergreen Californian lilac (ceanothus).

A different idea for using white comes from various grey and white gardens where it is used with grey or silver-grey foliage. This in turn opens up vistas of possibilities, such as white pinks with *Helichrysum splendidum* or white border carnations with garden ragwort (*Senecio laxifolius*) or the pure white roses of Virgo or Iceberg with sprays of *Senecio cineraria*.

Then we come to ideas for using different shades of one colour, sometimes in one flower. For example, in a large planting of gentians among *Gentiana sino-ornata* and *G. acaulis* I have seen a light Cambridge blue strain called Drake's strain. This was followed by the use of one colour to highlight another as in the case of blue with yellow. The pale yellow of *Thalictrum glaucum* with certain shades of blue delphiniums is a colour scheme that is worth remembering.

Such schemes can also be used in a garden if vivid colours are wanted, but perhaps would be more suitable for a flower arrangement (which can, after all, be changed often). In some gardens, where the softer tones of harmonizing colours are preferred, vivid contrasts of planting must be omitted.

One of the most usual arrangements of garden flowers might well be described as the 'mixed bunch'. There is a great deal of charm about a mixed garden bunch, arranged as naturally as possible. I have often heard it said at flower group meetings and discussions that what really gives the greatest pleasure is a bunch of flowers from the garden arranged as if they were picked in a basket. This does not necessarily mean that it must be a large arrangement, using a great quantity of flowers – far from it. But it does mean that the foliage of the garden is brought into the house and in this way a mixed bunch helps to forge a close link between gardening and flower arrangement. It is, after all, almost impossible to cut for the house without getting to know about such things as habitat, flowering time, lasting qualities, and structure of the plant. All this is of great value when arranging flowers, because respect for the material becomes more important than a dramatic effect.

The campanulas – in this case the Canterbury bell – belonging to one of the largest families of garden flowers are typical, in a bunch of mixed colours, of what one expects to find in a cottage herbaceous border. Often, their contribution is a sturdiness of stem, and *Campanula pyramidalis* especially gives height with a spire-like effect.

Naturally each garden will produce different material, but the fundamentals of an arrangement should be the same: a selection of tones of colour, shade and especially of shape. In this way one will have an interesting and economical decoration at any time of the year.

Perhaps a large vase of flowers is needed. Admittedly midsummer is a good time of the year to find material for such a group if one has

An arrangement of summer flowers, including lupins, poppies, sweet rocket, daisies, astrantia and so on. These are arranged in a marble pedestal vase which, being made of separate parts, can be used in a variety of heights

an established garden from which one can cut armfuls of flowers. But supposing this is not the case, and one is struggling to get a small border into running order from which basketfuls of material can ill be spared. How can a large colourful effect be achieved?

In the accompanying photograph there are a few bright poppies, two deep-toned peonies and two lupins with dark blue iris and some background material. The yellow peony is Alice Harding (Kinko) and the pink one Yackiyo-Tsubaki. These are precious plants which are just becoming established and so only now and again can one flower be spared. It is this kind of material which helps to give a bright and colourful effect in a large arrangement.

It will be seen that the group consists chiefly of leaves and flowers in green and white, and with enough of these to help out it is nearly always possible to make up a good-sized group without having to cut too heavily from a border which is not yet fully grown. Background material may vary according to what is already available either in the garden or in the way of wild flowers.

Green has always been acknowledged as a good background colour but with the addition of white it seems to become more vital and its original tones are intensified. The white is introduced by the ox-eye daisies, *Viburnum opulus* (or guelder rose), hedge parsley (or Queen Anne's lace), astrantia, cream-white foxgloves, *Phalaris arundinacea variegata* (or gardener's garters), and a touch of *Spiraea arguta* (or bridal wreath). The green is supplied by the foliage of most of the flowers – spiraea, viburnum, peony, gaultheria (or partridge berry), fern, *Tellima grandiflora* and one of the wild wood spurges.

The ox-eye daisies are usually available in the country but I find it is wise to have a clump somewhere in the garden. These smallish clear white flowers are invaluable. The more usually grown shasta daisies are also long-lasting, but they do not have quite the penetrating whiteness of these smaller, single ones. It is useful to have a clump of hedge parsley, too, in the garden.

The guelder rose is sturdy in growth, does not mind a north-facing situation and will soon grow rapidly enough to allow for cutting. The foliage turns a good colour in the autumn.

Astrantia is delicate in design and colouring but sturdy in its growth. On the whole it loves a cool, slightly shaded position, although I have seen it growing in a London garden in full sun. It lasts well as a cut flower. On account of its colouring and starlike shape it combines well with many different types of flower. The tall, thin spikes of *Tellima grandiflora* may be more difficult to see in the photograph. There is one between the deep pink lupin and a piece of fern and one next to the tallest poppy.

Ferns are nearly always good value, especially when they are seen clearly against a lighter background. When they first unfold from their tight fronds in the spring they may be rather too tender to use immediately, but they harden up later.

This is the time when many seedheads are ready for cutting,

particularly wild ones, and some of them look pretty arranged with fresh flowers. Heads of barley, oats and wheat, poppy heads, teasels and grasses can all give character and variety to a mixed arrangement. Here are some ideas:

A few of the small bulrushes with spikes of green water-grass, and towards the centre two heads of blue hydrangea, provide an economical and long-lasting group. A lightness is given to the bulrushes and hydrangeas by three sprays of golden privet.

Mignonette, verbascum and hydrangeas together make an interesting colour scheme of grey and green; the curving stems of the mignonette and the short side stems of verbascum will always add a graceful line to any arrangement. Mignonette could be grown from seed in a box or flowerpot if one has no garden – it is such a delightful plant that it is worth making an effort to have it. The hydrangea could be grown happily in a tub. When the flowers are finished the leaves go on for some time, and are still green and glossy when many other deciduous plants are over. For that reason alone it is worth growing.

Foliage too begins to come into its own. Arranged either alone or with a few fresh flowers, it can produce attractive line arrangements. Unfortunately one often has to have a garden to produce the necessary leaves and branches, though certain plants will grow in a very little space if there is a wall or fence for them to cling to.

A spray or two of clematis with trailing variegated periwinkle in a narrow-necked container is another idea for material from the garden, and polyantha roses make a colourful small arrangement.

In the photograph opposite grasses, reed mace and large arum leaves form a background for a few fresh flowers – in this case white phlox. These are hardy and half-hardy annual and perennial plants. The herbaceous phlox give pleasure in the late summer and early autumn months. The plants thrive in a semi-shady position and will be happier planted in a cool border with a north aspect than in the usual herbaceous border facing full sun. Pack them together closely with damp soil and plenty of rich feeding and wait for the glowing colours, or the purest white. They like plenty of water.

There are many fine varieties of *Phlox paniculata* including Frau Antonin Buchner, a reliable white; Rosenfeld, a mauve; Milly van Hoboken, a soft pink; Caroline van der Berg, blue; Lord Raleigh, violet; Mrs Kesselring, a rich purple; and a new introduction, Norah Leigh, is blue with variegated foliage.

Phlox will last quite well if they are cut when still in bud. They give warm tones of rose and lilac, or cool white, to a flower arrangement. Their scent is attractive to some people but not acceptable to others, so to be on the safe side, phlox should not be arranged on a dining table or in a position where they will be close at hand in a sitting-room. In a large group of flowers this scent will not be very obvious.

Scent is an important point to consider when preparing a table decoration. The perfume selected by a woman, whether in her bath,

Reed mace and grasses provide a background for the white phlox in this arrangement

A table arrangement of white lilies, roses and acanthus foliage together with sprays of *Cotinus coggygria atropurpurea* in a shallow, oval-shaped dish

her shampoo or in her cosmetics, is always quite rightly regarded as a personal matter. But why is this so? One might imagine after all that any good perfume would suit – why should individual selection be so important? Because, of course, no two people react in the same way to any particular scent and may even have exactly opposite tastes. In the matter of flowers there are conflicting opinions about the scent of nasturtiums, phlox and *Salvia turkestanica*, just to take three simple examples – and so it may be well to remember that the proximity of heavily scented flowers on a dining table might be rather overpowering, even unpleasant, or could clash with the delicious smell of good cooking.

The madonna lilies in this formal oblong group were only selected after some hesitation on account of their scent. But as green and white was required for a colour scheme and as the lilies were in prime condition at the time and only a few stems were used, it seemed a pity not to risk them. The group was needed for a formal dining table of some size so that by the time the other additions, such as glasses, cutlery and mats were in position, the flowers would not be in close proximity to those dining, and the scent, it is to be hoped, not too obvious.

The arrangement stands in an oblong Spode porcelain dish in white, banded with green. Only a small area of the green is seen but the white flowers show up better, I think, against the soft shade of green than if the container were completely white, and it is so often these small touches of colour which complete the whole effect. The roses are Félicité et Perpétue (all the better for being near-white) and their dark, glossy foliage makes an excellent background for them. Other foliage used consists of acanthus leaves, almost the same green, with two or three clusters of *Cotinus coggygria* (*Rhus cotinus*) *atropurpurea*. This deep wine-coloured foliage gives an additional depth of colour, varying the tones of the dark green from a dead· level of one dimension.

These arrangements are for different types of table during the summer months. The collection of mixed flowers from a July garden, arranged in a white jelly mould, was designed for a simple pine dining table. The colours include yellow, introduced by snapdragons, tight santolina flower heads, and the yellow and white of feverfew; white, in *Achillea ptarmica* The Pearl, *Viola septentrionalis* and clover; blue, represented by lavender and violas; various shades of red and pink by astilbe, polygonum, London pride, heuchera and roses; green by hart's tongue fern; and grey by *Helichrysum petiolatum*. Such a collection of flowers would blend in with any colour scheme and show up well against a light pine table top.

The white porcelain jelly mould is a gift for flower arranging, holding a small spray or a larger bunch equally well. It is especially useful for the times of year when only a few flowers are available and shows up short-stemmed gentians and yellow crocus with hepaticas and the first fresh green leaves of feverfew or wild arum in the spring. It may be arranged to form a coronet if a round shape is required or, as in the photograph, with longer-stemmed flowers at the sides to suit a narrow table.

These table decorations, different in their colour schemes, shape and choice of container, have one thing in common – their height. They are each about 15 cm (5 to 7 in) from the table. This question of height is another important point to consider when doing a flower arrangement for a dining table. We may have been a guest at a certain dinner or luncheon party where, for various reasons, the conversation has not flowed easily. Perhaps the guests have not met before and may have been slow to establish a point of contact. Such an occasion needs all the help available and would not be made easier by a tall, solid vase of flowers round which it was necessary to dodge in order to converse with someone across the table. Nothing which might contribute to the ease of individual guests and the enjoyment of the party should be overlooked, and a large flower arrangement can sometimes be a hindrance.

A group of mixed summer flowers in a white jelly mould for a dining table

The clematis in the photograph, with their delicate outline and colouring, provide a complete contrast to the formal green-and-white group on page 88, as well as the mixed group on page 89.

Where the lilies, roses and dark foliage produce an impression of solidity and, in the case of the lilies and the acanthus leaves, an almost sculptural outline, the twining stems of the clematis and their soft colouring give a more subtle effect.

The habit of clematis is almost the chief attraction of the plant, apart from the beauty of its flowers, and this may be exploited to the full in a table decoration. The clematis in the photograph are held in place by wire netting in a shallow Staffordshire dish. The deep purple variety with large flowers is Jackmanii; deep purple with small flowers, Etoile Violette; pink in varying shades to mauve, Comtesse de Bouchaud. All three varieties last well and are reasonably easy to grow. Although some of this family prefer lime in the soil, many will

A group of deep purple, light mauve and purple-blue clematis cut with some long stems, buds and foliage provides a table decoration

grow sturdily in an ordinary good soil if they have their roots in the shade and are allowed to climb up into the sun.

The *candidum* lilies may be more fussy about their growing conditions, some of them liking full sun, others partly shade, some preferring a heavy soil while others seem to thrive in sand and rubble. Once established they should multiply and none of them cares for being moved.

The mixed group is composed of flowers and leaves which do not generally demand special conditions, although it might be well to remember, if one is thinking of growing them, that astilbes (or spiraeas) like moisture. They will thrive by the edge of water, for instance, with their roots in damp soil.

Most people not only know how to grow sweet peas, but probably have their own special way of doing so. It is not necessary to relate the usual simple things about sowing a packet of seeds or trans-

planting seedlings outdoors in May, and the benefits of mulching and watering and staking. What seems to be important is the recent interest in the revival of the 'old sweet pea', sweetly scented and usually smaller flowered than the giants depicted on the seed packets.

Lathyrus odoratus is the original name of this species, and a very apt name it is if you believe, as I do, that scent is an essential of sweet peas. For anyone interested, Major J. F. Turral of Farnby, Yorkshire, has now collected together the largest number from various sources available in this country.

He wrote in an article published in the *RHS Journal*, January, 1965: 'There are, I think, a good many gardeners in this country who would grow the old sweet peas like a shot if they could get hold of them.' In the *Gardener's Chronicle* of January 29th, 1966, Mr Ian Unwin writes in the same strain, and mentions the interest aroused in them at the Trials Press Day, 1965. Large-sized flowers, frilliness and waved edges are not the true characteristics of the sweet pea, but the honey fragrance is.

Lathyrus latifolius, the everlasting pea, is most valuable for cutting. If allowed to scramble at will it is possible to cut long, twining branches (tendrils, flowers and buds, as well as leaves), which will lend themselves splendidly for decoration. The white variety The Pearl is almost better, although it may revert to the pinky-mauve colour of *L. latifolius* after a season or two. But it is worth having, even if it does. There are also pink and red varieties available from seedsmen.

Everyone knows the value of sweet peas for cutting and also that this is one certain instance when even the keenest gardener will tell us that cutting will do the plants good and we may help ourselves.

I would like to emphasize the real point of the particular group in the photograph opposite, which is to show sweet peas cut at some length so that it is possible to get height – not very considerable but, all the same, something taller than the usual length of stem associated with a bunch of sweet peas. This is done not by having sweet peas with enormous flowers at the ends of long, sturdy stems, but by cutting long lengths of the thick, columnar stems which bear the narrower stems for the flowers and which include tendrils and leaves. Obviously this can only be done if there are some good-sized clumps of sweet peas to cut at, but if so, the leaves and tendrils make a most delicate and suitable frame for the delicate flowers, showing them up as individual flowers, and avoiding the massed effect of a tight bunch.

To give extra support to the stems the large-mesh wire netting was bunched up as high as possible in the centre of the group.

On a hot summer's day, a vase of carefully selected flowers is not only beautiful but makes the room seem cooler, however sultry the temperature. To achieve this effect the best colour combination

A large bunch of sweet peas in mixed colours cut with long stems, tendrils and buds to show the full grace of their habit

The glass bulb vase is a good green to show off the cream-white roses and the flowers of myrtle. Fennel and *Alchemilla mollis* flowers add further variations to the colour scheme of green and cream

is probably green and white: either a handful of green leaves in a white container, or white flowers arranged with foliage, grasses or unripened seedheads.

Nor should we forget the infinite possibilities of green on its own, which can sometimes be used in varying depths and tones of colour, sometimes as a contrast or a background.

First let us consider some of the many shades of green, varying not only in degree of colour, but also in texture. For instance, it is interesting to notice that a rough-surfaced leaf (foxglove and anchusa, for example) although in itself the same dark green tone as a smooth one (ivy for instance), will look several degrees lighter than the other. Some hollies, although all are smooth, are considerably lighter in tone than others.

There are several leaves including *Viburnum tinus*, laurel, camellia, berberis, escallonia and some holly, which might be described correctly as 'dark' green, but all vary, not only between each other, but between individual shrubs. The fresh shoots on a rhododendron are in complete contrast with the older leaves, and the same applies to most of the other evergreens mentioned.

And then there are the leaves of border plants, sometimes overshadowed by their flowers and not always fully appreciated.

A lupin leaf, for example, is dramatic and unusual, with its fan-like shape; young poppy leaves, early in a fresh green, rather fussy along their serrated edge; delphinium leaves, dark or light in colour; *Alchemilla mollis*, with the added attraction of a raindrop after a heavy shower; bergenia, in all sizes and shades of green; astrantia, wide and indented; and hosta, sometimes in a clear green, sometimes in a blue-grey green, now and then variegated with a margin of cream, or patches of cream towards the centre, surrounded by a fairly wide edging of green.

Which brings me to the large selection of variegated leaves, usually off-white, yellow, or cream with green. Well-known examples are golden privet and variegated periwinkles, holly, figwort, weigela, false fig (*Fatsia japonica*), elaeagnus and euonymus.

The reference to elaeagnus reminds me of silver-backed leaves such as lavender, rosemary, willow, *Senecio cineraria* (*Cineraria maritima*) and *S. laxifolius*. The silvery-grey foliage of *Senecio cineraria* often appears as a green leaf after a heavy fall of rain, and so might reasonably be included in such an arrangement.

The green bulb glass provides useful anchorage for a mixed bunch of various leaves and flowers in tones of green, white and cream. This vase is identical with the one illustrated earlier, on page 41, in a different colour.

The flowers here include branches of the enchanting shrub myrtle, with its dark pointed leaves as a sturdy background for its sparkling creamy-white flowers. There are also sprays of fennel foliage – fluffy and soft – and the yellow-green of *Alchemilla mollis* flowers. Iceberg roses in bud and Madame Alfred Carrière (fully out) carry on the

theme of cream-white against a clear green, giving the emphasis of larger flowers towards the centre of the group.

Looking again at flowers in a glass vase in the photograph opposite the branches of hop flowers provide a contrast with the tobacco plant nicotiana, and the stems seen through the tall, slender vase give an added balance to the rather drooping shape of the arrangement.

The hop flowers are a light, rather delicate shade of green, but later on, as they dry on the plant, they may turn either a light buff colour or a deeper russet, both of which are most useful for a dried arrangement throughout the winter months.

The charm of transparency is especially evident in this group. The stems, delicate in colouring and texture, can be seen clearly.

The hop flowers are so delicate that it is sometimes difficult to find a vase which is not too heavy and solid in contrast. Glass is the perfect answer, especially something simple in design to set off the fussiness of the flowers.

When a tall arrangement is called for, there is something to be said for using a narrow glass Victorian vase like the one in the photograph. Such containers are not always easy to find and are not, of course, suitable for all occasions, but there are times when their height can be important and can add to the size of the group.

If one has been fortunate enough to find such a vase, perhaps in an antique or a second-hand furniture shop, there are two points to remember. The first is that the water level naturally falls rather quickly in the narrow neck.

The second point is that the inside of the glass must be kept clean and this can often be rather troublesome. A good way of keeping it clean is to shred two or three large sheets of tissue paper into small pieces and to shake these up inside in the water after allowing them to soak in it for some time.

A vase of this kind may be stood on the floor or on a low pedestal.

A hop is a climbing plant of great vigour. Not unlike a vine in appearance until it bursts out into flower, it can be a valuable addition to decoration. With its hanging green clusters and curving stems, it is in itself decorative while it is still growing, especially when climbing up into a trellis or pergola, so that the broad leaves may be seen to advantage.

Once established it will grow 'like a weed' and may then have to be pruned severely. Plant during the spring, topdress with manure, water freely in hot weather and cut down the plants after flowering in the autumn.

Propagation is by the division of roots in spring. It is quite easy to keep a plant under control in a smallish garden if the new shoots are thinned out as they appear, allowing only the leaders to get away. This will also strengthen them and provide more luxuriant foliage.

For some reason or other, geraniums (or pelargoniums) are some-

Branches of hop flowers with lime green and white nicotianas

Pelargoniums are arranged here in a
shallow dish. Often thought of as a pot-
plant flower, they are of great value for
cutting, introducing a variation of
colouring both in their flowers and in
their foliage

times only thought of in connection with window-boxes, tubs, patio
gardening or bedding out and not at all from the point of view of
cutting for flower arrangement. Strictly speaking, these plants which
we always think of as bedding geraniums are, in fact, pelargoniums;
the true geranium is a hardy herbaceous perennial and quite a different plant.

Pelargoniums are invaluable for decoration, not only for the varied
colours of their flowers – scarlet, palest pink, mauve, crimson, cerise,
red, salmon, and white – but also for their foliage.

The leaves have different shapes and colourings, from the rather
pointed deep green of the ivy-leaved pelargonium and the feathery
lighter green of the scented *Pelargonium graveolens* to the rounded,
and sometimes striped, foliage of the *Pelargonium zonale*, with circles
of white, yellow or bronze.

It has always seemed to me that the value of white pelargoniums
has been under-rated. For an all-white group, perhaps a table decoration, there can be few more suitable flowers to arrange in a white
container, perhaps with Iceberg roses and short sprays of anaphalis,
sweet rocket or achillea. White *Nigella damascena* (love-in-a-mist) is
a perfect foil for the rounded shape of a white geranium – a most
attractive one is Modesty (introduced from the United States), which
has a slight tint of palest pink.

Then there are all the possibilities of 'clashing' reds or toning pinks.
Bright reds and orange-reds make a good splash of colour, while the
softer shades of pink, cerise and lilac arranged together are more
restful. Contrast can be achieved in the red group by the addition of
deep blue anemones, delphiniums or anchusa and, if a lighter blue is
required, by forget-me-nots or blue nigella.

Highly recommended as a pure scarlet is the old Victorian
favourite, Paul Crampel. An equally sturdy outdoor grower is
Decorator. Although they may not be so sturdy, all the Irene types
are good for cutting, and Irene and Penny Irene put together would
produce a cheerful group. Constance Spry frequently grew
pelargoniums for cutting and used to write of the effect of 'clashing
reds' obtainable in many different varieties.

She also mentioned the lasting properties of pelargoniums. 'There
is an idea that geraniums do not last well,' she wrote. 'It is true that
the full-blown flower drops its petals at a touch, but all the buds open
in water and fill up the gaps as the older flowers fade.' I have, from
personal experience, found this to be true.

The leaves of *Pelargonium zonale* offer a wide selection of colour
schemes, quite apart from the colour of the flowers. Of this classifica-
tion Mrs Henry Cox is well known. The leaf, with which we are all
familiar when thinking in terms of pelargoniums, is rounded with
veins leading down from the centre to the crinkly edge.

The foliage of the scented geranium, *Pelargonium graveolens*, is a
fresh green with no markings, but deeply indented. A plant with a
delicate outline, it is a contrast to the heavy, solid shape of

Pelargonium zonale and provides the flower arranger with 'quite a different type of material.

Nicotianas are favourite flowers, amongst so many favourites, chiefly on account of their elusive scent and the starry whiteness of their white flowers. They come, of course, in many colours, but chiefly in mauves, purples and dark reds, as well as green. Not necessarily an autumn flower, yet they linger on in a kindly way quite late into the time of chrysanthemums, to lighten the burden of retiring summer.

An extra attraction is the foliage in a fresh green, and if it is cut with as many leaves as possible on the long stem – frequently the bigger leaves come low down towards the roots – together with some of the buds, this all adds to the character of the plant and the interest of the arrangement. I have cut it for a tall group in late autumn when I was grateful for its feeling of summer and the way that it goes on much later than most other flowers.

People are inclined to think that because of their rather fragile appearance these flowers are not long-lasting. However, they are, in fact, most reliable, even to the extent of lasting for at least a fortnight (in the cooler weather), as long as the dying flowers are taken off to allow the young buds to come on.

Nicotiana is treated as an annual, half-hardy, which once established goes on through summer well into the autumn. It grows in ordinary soil and will flourish in sun or semi-shade, and will only sometimes survive the winter in well-drained, sheltered gardens. It usually must be renewed each spring, either by young plants obtained from a nurseryman, or seeds should be sown early in a warm frame or greenhouse. But the plants must not be put out until all danger of frost is over.

On account of its sweet scent on summer evenings it should be placed close to the house, although much of its attraction is not only the fragrance of the flowers at this time of day but also their shining whiteness which gleams in the evening light and, because of their shape, gives a starlike effect.

For cutting, these flowers are magnificent. Their foliage is a lush green and a good shape, and there is plenty of it. When the stalks are cut to their full extent, this usually provides excellent material for a tall arrangement (see page 96) as much of the beauty lies in the leaves.

The most useful of the tobacco plants is probably *Nicotiana alata* (*N. affinis*), a handsome plant indeed when it has grown to its full height of $1\frac{1}{4}$ to $1\frac{1}{2}$ m (4 to 5 ft). The flowers are creamy white and have the most exquisite perfume. A strain known as Sensation Mixed produces shades of red, pink, mauve, as well as white. There is also a variety, Lime Green, which has green flowers and these are a subtle colour useful in certain arrangements. As they all flower well on into early autumn they have been most valuable in Harvest Festival decorations. Constance Spry mentions arranging the purple variety in an autumn group with grapes and mauve dianthus and 'used it a good deal for the decoration of the house'.

White nicotianas contrasted against the dark colouring of a lustre teapot. These are flowers which smell sweetly and last well

Pale blue agapanthus flowers blend with lysimachia and *Buddleia crispa* in a grey and white colour scheme on a windowsill

Although we have become greatly interested in flower work during the last fifty years, there still sometimes seems to be too much emphasis on the size and quantity of material, and perhaps not enough respect for a few flowers and leaves arranged in as natural a way as possible. Stunts and displays are all very well occasionally but they are not easy to live with. Mr Robert Graves, speaking in a radio programme, said: 'The test of a painting is not what it looks like in an exhibition frame on varnishing day; the test is whether it can hang on the wall in your dining-room a year or two later after you bought it, without going dead on you. The test of a poem is whether you can reread it with excitement three years after the critics tell you it's a masterpiece.' The test of style and design in flower arrangement seems to be on these lines – whether it is simple and natural and easy to live with. Respect, love for the material, and humility must all contribute to its composition.

The capacity for being able to select material and display it unostentatiously, it may be argued, depends on the personal taste of the arranger. Of course this is so, and it would possibly be wise to consider the part played by personal taste in flower arrangement.

Perhaps the most important thing about taste is that it should be individual and that it can be developed. By being interested in other branches of art, by studying glass, porcelain, furniture, fabric designs, wallpapers, quite apart from painting, music, sculpture, we become more in tune with line and colour and form. The critical sense expands and one learns, too, what to accept and appreciate and what to discard, and even a small knowledge of any of these arts will be of help when studying another.

A sense of awareness and an appreciation of detail in our day-to-day life – the sights and sounds around us – may help to develop this discrimination almost as much as concentrated study in an art gallery.

Here is a natural-looking group in gentle colours placed in good light by a window.

When cutting a delicate-toned flower like this buddleia for the house there are a few important points to consider. First, perhaps, comes the necessity for a simple container, and secondly, for a plain background for the arrangement. This applies more especially, of course, when the buddleia branches are used alone, but they are also suitable for arranging with other flowers, particularly when a lighter effect is required with heavy material. The leaves are a good silver-grey as well as being decorative in the way in which they are arranged on the stem.

Apart from its many other qualities, this buddleia (*Buddleia crispa*) lasts well and is easy to grow once it gets established. It seems to like sun and shelter from the wind but is not fussy as to soil.

The white flowers of *Lysimachia clethroides* on their slim curving stems also give grace and distinction, as well as a clear outline, to other more bushy flowers.

Dahlias are popular flowers for arrangements and come in a great

variety of colours, types and sizes, but I write of them with some diffidence as I never feel absolutely certain of their lasting qualities. There are some occasions when it is possible to use flowers which may or may not let you down, and I know that there are many dahlias which are completely dependable, but all the same I'm afraid I still have this feeling of uncertainty, although I have found the smaller pompon type of dahlia to last well even when arranged on a pinholder.

I would prefer, for instance, if doing a large wedding group or altar vases in church, to depend on something else to provide an important colour note.

This may seem unjust to a noble, widely loved flower, but one must write from personal experience and mine, with dahlias, has not always been fortunate. I hasten, in fairness, to add that I understand that in official flower arrangement circles this is not the general consensus of opinion.

Dahlias come into the category of flowers that can be arranged alone and yet provide a variety of colour in the same way as zinnias, carnations, some sweet peas and some roses. The colours range from pure white, clear lemon yellow and fiery orange, through shades of apricot, tangerine and burnt sienna to deep copper, bronze, and dark red, not to mention the various tones of pink and mauve which are also available.

Dahlias are like zinnias in their variety of colour (only not, to my mind, of such depth and intensity of shade and tone). They also come from Mexico. There are many categories in garden varieties, some of them called star dahlias, others anemone-flowered dahlias, while others include cactus dahlias, pompon dahlias, peony-flowered dahlias and decorative dahlias. Having made a selection from pages of nurserymen's lists, it is then important to discover the conditions they prefer and to follow instructions for lifting them in the late autumn.

Dahlias are rich feeders and like a deep, moist soil, well drained, and preferably not under trees, for despite the fact that they are often recommended for growing in contrast against dark-leaved shrubs, they do not like to be over-shadowed by branches. Here again, they are similar to zinnias, and do best in a sunny position. If the soil is naturally light and inclined to dry out, liquid manure must be added and watering is essential when the young plants are first put out into the garden during May.

In case of danger from late frosts after planting, the dahlias may be protected by upturned flower pots at night. Owing to the weight of the flowers and the quantity of heavy foliage, buds, and stems, the plants are likely to need individual staking. To ensure that the soil is kept moist they should be well mulched once they are established, but it is of great importance that if and when this is done, the soil underneath is not allowed to become dry. One of the best ways of keeping the soil in a suitable condition is to go over the bed lightly with a hoe, so as not to injure the tubers.

Copper-coloured dahlias cut short to give a deep effect towards the centre against the lighter background of montbretia are arranged here in a contrasting blue bulb glass

Roses

A collection of roses seems to me like a book of favourite cooking recipes or an anthology of poems – the choice should be personal, reflecting the taste of the owner.

There has always been a certain amount of controversy about arranging roses. Some people say that it is a waste of time to cut them for the house as they drop quickly and therefore look better growing in the garden.

Others contend that they give extra work as they have to be renewed more quickly than other flowers. Some find them difficult to cut and arrange on account of the thorns – and anyone who has ever tried to arrange Albertine roses will no doubt agree with this. And so, one way or another, roses come in for a good deal of criticism.

But in spite of this there is the fact that the rose has been one of the best loved of all flowers for some hundreds of years, whatever its lasting qualities might be, and from the time of Chaucer onwards it has been a familiar subject in poetry and in painting.

In fact, there are roses that fade quickly when they are cut, but there are others that last for some days, and with such a well-loved flower it seems worth while taking the trouble to find out which are especially suitable for cutting for the house.

Perhaps it would be as well, before going into some detail about individual roses, to emphasize again the few well-known but most important points to think of when cutting roses of any kind to ensure that they will last as long as possible.

First, they should be cut in fairly tight bud and at a cool time of the day. Then the base of their stems should be split or crushed, perhaps a few of the lower leaves and any thorns cut off. Give them a deep drink of water before arranging. Some roses like to have the whole of their stem stripped so that they can drink more easily up the length of the stalk.

I have known cases where this last treatment was applied to a bunch of the small, pink Carol roses resulting in the group lasting for nearly three weeks. This also applies to the Garnette rose. Both these roses are sold by many florists throughout much of the year. Like most other flowers, roses resent too sharp an alteration in temperature and dislike a draught.

The removal of the thorns can often prove to be a lengthy business as well as an uncomfortable one with certain roses.

Personally, I think roses are well worth the trouble and time if one has them at hand in the garden and if cut when still in bud, their life will at least be somewhat prolonged.

A large group of roses will need a certain amount of replenishing. But it is possible to do this without taking the whole arrangement to pieces by cutting off the dead roses and adding newly opening buds just where the old blooms have been.

A splash of sunshine introduced by a few Golden Showers roses arranged with their buds and gleaming green foliage

It is important, I think, when tidying up a bowl of roses, not to try to take out the whole stem – anyone having done so will no doubt remember how much all the other stems become entangled.

The astonishing increase in 'perpetual' roses, as opposed to garden roses which only flowered once during the summer, was noted by Dean Hole of Rochester in 1891. The Dean had instigated the first National Rose Show in 1858, when there were only two roses which could be counted as perpetuals. By 1891 there were about five thousand.

In those days perpetual meant flowering twice, but nowadays many gardeners will only select and order roses which flower right through the summer and in some cases into late autumn.

The arrangement on the opposite page was photographed in midsummer and includes Albertine, a climber with a reasonably short flowering period. But there are also Penelope, Paul's Scarlet and Iceberg, which can be relied upon to produce a continuously vigorous show of blooms, only now and again pausing for a rest.

All rose lovers have their favourites, and I must confess that my own selection does not only include many perpetuals. If a rose like Madame Pierre Oger, Céleste or Fantin Latour provides me with its enchanting flowers only once in a flowering season, I am more than grateful. However, the fact is that, while these varieties are not among the constant long-flowering ones, they do bloom again at intervals (especially if the dead flower heads are cut off), although not in great profusion. Madame Pierre Oger, especially, goes on gallantly and I have had flowers as late as October.

Of the perpetuals shown here, Penelope has quantities of deep cream buds, large flowers with bright yellow stamens and stout, well-defined dark green leaves. The first roses usually come at the beginning of June and continue in some profusion for a few weeks. Then comes a period of rest followed by more flowers. These go on into the autumn. Penelope is of most vigorous growth and will make a good hedge about 6 ft high. The flowers are always in clusters and if the first one is cut off when it is over, the other buds will take its place.

The clear, honest red of Paul's Scarlet is well known. It is a reliable rose, giving plenty of flowers on and off during the summer, and has a good, sturdy growth. Although classified as a rambler, it is more like a climber in habit.

Iceberg is a splendid rose in many respects. It has tall, straight stems and shining green foliage. The long buds are usually slightly flushed with pink but open out into clear white flowers, with almost a pale green tinge. These come first in June and continue until the winter when they are only defeated by the bad weather. There are large beds of Iceberg in Queen Mary's rose garden, Regent's Park, London. It is an ideal variety for arranging. In the photograph numerous buds and rather light-coloured leaves are on a curving stem at the top of the group.

Paul's Scarlet roses in a low bowl

A collection of old roses

Facing page: Various roses – chiefly Albertine – arranged formally in a contemporary container, supported by their own foliage, stems and buds

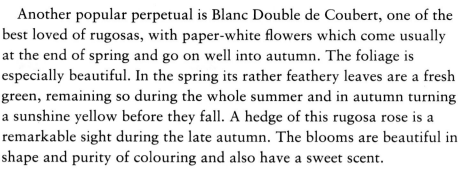

Another popular perpetual is Blanc Double de Coubert, one of the best loved of rugosas, with paper-white flowers which come usually at the end of spring and go on well into autumn. The foliage is especially beautiful. In the spring its rather feathery leaves are a fresh green, remaining so during the whole summer and in autumn turning a sunshine yellow before they fall. A hedge of this rugosa rose is a remarkable sight during the late autumn. The blooms are beautiful in shape and purity of colouring and also have a sweet scent.

This group consists of Stanwell Perpetual roses and tall stems of polygonum with a few Cécile Brunner roses, white potentilla, and London pride. These are arranged in large-mesh wire netting, raised up to give extra support to the longer stems, in a chromium holder (this could also be used as a candlestick, with short flowers at its base). Such containers can be bought from most florists.

The curving branches, tight buds and clusters of small, well-defined leaves are all part of the charm of the Stanwell Perpetual rose which flowers profusely early in the summer; it is less energetic during the height of summer and then has another, most welcome, burst of flowering in October. Cécile Brunner is one of the early-flowering roses – some people say it comes out as early as April, but from my own experience I would say the beginning of May. In Murrell's catalogue this rose is described as having 'large sprays of miniature flesh-pink flowers of exquisite shape – a gem'.

The tall pink spikes of the polygonum grow up well above their thick, spreading leaves and are most helpful in giving extra height where there is only space for thin-stemmed flowers. This polygonum is valuable indeed for cutting and easy to grow; it rather enjoys a damp situation.

London pride, with its small distinctive pink-and-white flowers, is one of my favourites. It adds lightness and delicate charm to most groups and also lasts quite well. The little white potentilla is another favourite, flowering its head off once it is established.

Summer is the time for roses. They are blooming in the garden, tended and trimmed and cosseted. They are rambling amongst the hawthorn and hazels in the hedgerows, scented, radiant and wild.

There is ample evidence of the affection and interest with which roses have been regarded for many years. Books have been written about them, and pictures of them painted.

In poetry from Chaucer to Shakespeare, from George Herbert to Robert Burns the beauty of the rose has been portrayed. There is hardly a garden without one, or a gardener who has not grown one.

Perhaps the most important point about arranging roses is the same as when growing them, that is to have affection for them. As Dean Hole writes in *A Book About Roses*: 'He who would have beautiful roses in his garden . . . must love them well and always'.

Roses Stanwell Perpetual and Cécile Brunner arranged in a candlestick holder. Large-mesh wire netting is used to give them extra support

Autumn Arrangements

Somehow, towards the end of summer, nature seems to take a deep breath in the garden to become more radiant and colourful. Hot sultry weather may have drained all brightness from the leaves, making them appear more solid and heavy than at any other time of the year, almost lifeless. And then follows this refreshing period, when light and shade are apparent again and there is a liveliness amongst the leaves and flowers before autumn settles down.

Zinnias are, perhaps, of all flowers the most characteristic of this time of year when the transition comes between summer and autumn. They glow in many jewel colours of bronze, orange, flame and clear yellow to the softer shades of clear pink or a deep lilac or even a green-white, and form the basis of this group. It should be admitted, I think, that there are occasionally some zinnia stems which flop and then the whole flower head droops owing to its weight. If this happens it may be advisable to cut the stem much shorter.

Because these flowers have so much colour in themselves they can look especially attractive with soft-coloured seedheads or leaves, such as green and purple teasels, fresh green hop flowers, *Alchemilla mollis* foliage, mignonette, sweet corn or green poppy heads. There is nothing like a cluster of *Senecio cineraria* White Diamond or a few sprays of the curry plant to emphasize a glowing colour. The rather felt-like leaves of *Phlomis fruticosa* are also useful although less dramatic.

Other foliage of varying tones and shades includes branches of dark green cistus – excellent in its definite outline; one large leaf of *Fatsia japonica* tucked in towards the centre, and a spray of *Parrotia persica* introducing a hint of autumn with its tawny, crisp leaves. A blue-green note is provided by the small, tufty foliage of rue.

Depth of colouring comes with heliotrope in rich purple, sometimes still affectionately known as 'cherry pie'. *Cotoneaster horizontalis* provides an interesting contrast in outline as well as the bright red of its berries against the dark green leaves.

Perhaps the most important contribution to such a mixed bunch is the addition of white flowers. There are only three white single flowers and two or three stems of cream-white anaphalis but these are enough to highlight the various tones and colourings ranging from pale green and soft mauve and pink to the strong oranges, yellows and reds. As many people have discovered when faced with clashing colours, the introduction of white can often solve any problems in this connection. The cerise zinnia is saved in this case by

A mixed group of early autumn flowers arranged in a black urn. Amongst these are grey-white anaphalis, purple spikes of mint, zinnias, dahlias, nicotianas and deep purple heliotrope (cherry pie)

112

the lime green of the nicotianas and the white chrysanthemum lightens the orange-red zinnia and the deep yellow of the spray chrysanthemums.

In the autumn our gardens shine with a variety of flowers different from some of those that were out in the months of high summer, and the flower shops are filled with blooms of every conceivable shape, size, scent and colour.

For one of my arrangements I have chosen tobacco plants (nicotiana), which come in many different colours. They are arranged here in a wine glass.

It is interesting to discover that the choice of flowers has not always been so great as it is today, and that perhaps only as far back as one hundred and fifty years ago the selection was limited by comparison. It may be that we take this present richness of plants and shrubs too much for granted, because we are used to seeing them and have probably known them all our lives.

Some of the cottage garden flowers, which include special favourites such as dog's tooth violets, winter aconites, grape hyacinths and the madonna lily, were mentioned by Gerard in his catalogue of 1596. Sweet rocket is one of the flowers listed by the Rev. William Hanbury about the middle of the 18th century, and mignonette and love-in-a-mist were first mentioned many years earlier.

These flowers followed from the herb gardens of the monasteries and provided the corner stones on which many gardens have been built. They are our joy and pride; but the expansion and development of gardens today has been made possible only by the more recent introduction of plants from foreign countries.

Many of these introductions were the result of the courage and perseverance of the plant pioneers, who risked their health and personal safety. Expeditions were made into uncharted areas, and sometimes they disappeared for months on end. Men crossed glaciers and snow-covered mountain peaks, were attacked by wild animals, and suffered extremes of climate.

I am thinking of such people as David Douglas, Robert Fortune and E. H. Wilson. Looking upon the beauty of a *Lilium regale*, with its dark green stem and thin, curving leaves, its cluster of pure white flowers, backed with streaks of pink, its heavy yellow stamens and its exotic scent, one should recall Ernest Henry Wilson, who found the plant in China in 1910. He was travelling in a sedan chair at the time and without any warning a landslide came crashing down from the mountains. Wilson was flung down a steep slope towards a river and badly injured.

We also owe much to David Douglas, who brought back or sent home to England from America many pine trees, the Douglas fir, berberis, snowberry, flowering currant, garrya, clarkia and *Lupinus polyphyllus*, from which our modern lupins are descended. He lost his life exploring in the Hawaiian Islands.

One of the botanists he met while plant finding on the eastern side

Nicotianas contrasting both in shape and colouring with the pink spikes of polygonum and the soft green of mignonette

of the Rockies was Thomas Drummond, in whose honour *Phlox drummondii* was named. This plant afterwards became so rare in its native home that it had to be reintroduced into American gardens.

Flowers of the autumn include the dahlia, from Mexico, and the chrysanthemum, from China. It was first thought that the dahlia tuber might be used as a food. This idea was not developed, but the flower became a great favourite with the Empress Josephine, who cultivated it in her gardens at Malmaison.

Chrysanthemums were first known to flower in this country in the Chelsea Physic Garden in 1794, but they were lost for some time afterwards. They reappeared in force during the 19th century, the pompon variety being brought by Robert Fortune, whose errand on this occasion had been to take China tea into India.

Many flowers that we enjoy today in our gardens and are able to cut for the house have stories of courage and fortitude behind them. We should remember gratefully those men as we walk round the garden cutting a curving branch or a lovely bud.

Nicotianas – or tobacco plants – came originally from South Brazil. In this wine glass they are cut quite short and arranged with polygonum with its sparkling red flowers. Both these plants are good for cutting and last well. The polygonum comes from the Himalayas, and is one of the most sturdy of all garden plants – in fact some people find it too invasive. It seems at its best in an isolated position.

Featured in the group opposite is anaphalis and rue. Anaphalis is a hardy perennial, one of the *Compositae* family and a charming plant, usually rather small with silver-grey foliage and silver-white flowers. It grows well in most positions but prefers a sunny border. Anaphalis should be planted in autumn or spring and may be propagated by division in the autumn or spring. Seeds may be sown outdoors in the spring.

As its common name suggests, it is one of the everlasting flowers which are sometimes regarded with suspicion by some gardeners. Perhaps they feel that these kinds of plant give an artificial atmosphere in the border on account of the nature of their flowers. This may apply to certain kinds of helichrysum, in fact I think it does, especially to those which look as if they are made of paper or have been heavily varnished, but the anaphalis does not give the same kind of impression. The flowers are small, white, or white and yellow, pretty in bud and also when they are fully out. Depending on the state at which they are cut, in bud or wide open, they give an impression of either white, grey-white, or yellow and white. This is one of the smallest of the whole *Compositae* family and to anyone fond of daisies it is quite irresistible.

In the border this plant provides the touch of white and yellow described during the late summer months. It may be cut and arranged when it is fresh or kept until later when it will be of great value in a dried arrangement. There is no actual drying to be done, as it dries off itself.

The leaves of rue are delicate in shape, soft blue-green in colour, and have an unusual scent. They go on bravely through the winter and are always at hand to provide something attractive for a small arrangement of flowers.

There is probably a greater diversity of opinion over the scent of the leaves than on any other garden scent. So often something that appeals to one person is unpleasant to another. Mr Jason Hill wrote: 'I may say, for example, that rue, if it is lightly handled, smells of coconut; but the comparison is by no means exact, and the reader may consider it more like gorse, ripe apricots, or cowslips, for all these scents have something in common'. (Jason Hill, *The Curious Gardener*. Faber & Faber, 1932.) The question of scent is an important point to consider when arranging a small bunch of flowers which may stand at one's elbow on an occasional table or in a visitor's bedside vase.

Rue will grow easily in most soils, so long as it is in full sun. It should also have a sheltered position, coming as it does from southern Europe. I have it growing near the top of a low wall but sheltered by bergenia and a large cistus.

Let us bring the colour of sunshine into the house in the autumn,

Senecio cineraria arranged with the blue-grey foliage of rue and the grey-white of anaphalis

doubly welcome after the grey skies, dark evenings and solid rain-storms of approaching winter have begun.

The colours of flowers do more than anything to bring this 'burst of sunshine' indoors. Chrysanthemums come in all shades of yellow, and they last well. However, it is always advisable to split the stems immediately before arranging as this ensures that they will be capable of a greater intake of water. It may also be helpful to give them a deep drink in a bucket of water first even if they are cut straight from the garden or bought freshly from a reliable florist.

Perhaps here I may make a suggestion for including short sprays of a variegated shrub.

Golden privet is an old friend providing that particular sunshine yellow unobtainable in almost any other material, sometimes reviled for its mundane characteristics but often championed by gardeners who have learnt to value it.

Some sixty years ago Miss Gertrude Jekyll wrote in her book *Flower Decoration in the House*: 'There are several shrubs with variegated foliage that are of great use in winter decorations. One of the best of these is the gold-variegated privet, holding its leaves till well after Christmas . . .' and in *Colour Schemes for the Flower Garden* she recommends it as 'one of the few shrubs that have a place in the flower border. Its clean, cheerful, bright yellow gives a note of just the right colour all through the summer.'

More recently, in the *Gardeners' Chronicle*, Mr Will Ingwersen writes in one of his many charming and erudite articles (this one especially written for flower arrangers): 'Equally valuable, when allowed to grow naturally, is the golden-leaved privet, *Ligustrum ovalifolium aureum*. *Ligustrum ovalifolium variegatum* is sometimes offered as a substitute but, for the special needs of flower arrangers, it is inferior.'

Now a word about the container for this small group. It seems to me well worth while – and not necessarily extravagant – to select a container suitable only for certain colours, if it is attractive in itself. It is stimulating to think out something new to go well with it and possibly to discover material that one had not thought of using before. An example of this in the group opposite is the sauceboat or gravy dish with a decoration round the brim and round the base in brown and yellow. This might reasonably be considered restricting but, in fact, the dish was just right for this collection of sunshine colours, and in the summer it was well suited to a bunch of butter-cups, creamy-yellow honeysuckle and sprays of yellow broom.

This is an obvious case of the choice of container dictating not only the shape of the arrangement but also the colour.

The sprays of mignonette are particularly suitable to this design and colour scheme. Strictly a perennial, mignonette is normally grown as an annual. It likes sunny beds or the front of borders or rock gardens and will grow well in ordinary soil. The seeds should be sown where they will eventually flower, and thinned out after

Mignonette picks up the colours of the brighter pelargoniums, begonias and chrysanthemums in this sauceboat group

reaching a height of about $2\frac{1}{2}$ cm (1 in). Water freely during hot summer weather.

Mignonette, with its soft, rather subtle perfume, and its green and slightly coppery flowers, is surely one of the most charming and unusual plants to grow in the garden or to cut for flower arrangement in the house. It has been grown and loved for many years and still it holds its own with more brightly coloured, larger introductions, perhaps on account of its quiet appearance. As a cut flower its lasting properties might almost be considered the most important quality, as it will go on in water happily for nearly three weeks.

There are different types of mignonette, some of them with a good perfume and some with less. Miss Jekyll had harsh things to say about the newer 'novelties' which were sometimes without scent or had too reddish a flower: 'For mignonette is and always should be a plant of modest colouring and sweetest scent . . .' (Gertrude Jekyll, *A Gardener's Testament*. Country Life, 1937.) Among those listed are the following: Orange Queen, Triumph, Crimson Giant slightly taller at 45 cm ($1\frac{1}{2}$ ft), and a white-flowering variety, White Pearl. I have no personal knowledge of Crimson Giant but feel that the name here is wrong for what should be quite a small flower.

If bushy plants with a large number of flowers are required, the shoots should be taken out as the plant grows so that the side branches will give good crops. The ground in which the seeds are sown should be well trodden down before sowing.

A vase of flowers is required for a low table. What points does one have to consider?

Here we look into a low terra-cotta dish filled with small flowers. It is shallow but has enough depth of water for short stems. A clump of broken-up moss is their only anchorage. This small group can really be regarded in terms of the peaceful relaxation that flower arrangement is sometimes claimed to be. In the first place it is better to sit down to do it and, secondly, there need be no preconceived plan or anxiety about fitting in with closely surrounding objects.

All one's attention can be given to the charm of the individual flowers: the cheerful orange of the tagetes, the clear yellow of the pot marigolds (calendula) and the soft green of the fennel. If further green is required at this time, there are the interesting leaves of bergenia and the ladder fern. Almost opposites in outline and texture, the bergenia leaves are flat, rounded and leathery, and those of the ladder fern crinkled, almost silky, narrow and pointed. They show each other up well or provide an interesting contrast in the same type of arrangement. Obviously the large, full-grown leaves would be out of proportion to the kind of flowers shown in this photograph.

Ladder fern reminds me of a book (published by Hutchinson) called *The Victorian Fern Craze*, by David Elliston Allen. It is a fascinating history of how ferns were grown in the 19th century and deals with the development of the Wardian case and the introduction of greenhouse and hothouse plants.

Mr Allen quotes *The Gardeners' Chronicle* of 1856 as commenting on the fact that the Royal Horticultural Society's garden was to have a fernery: 'Lovers of plants begin to prefer graceful form to mere spots of colour . . .' said the writer of the editorial.

Perhaps the Victorians were over-enthusiastic in the matter of ferns, but today these could receive more attention without any danger of exaggeration.

Having suggested that this group might be arranged while one is sitting down, I would like to mention a piece of equipment useful in flower arranging, which is a dustsheet. This not only protects the immediate surfaces and the floor, but provides a space where one can lay out the material and see at a glance exactly what is there, while the odd leaves, ends of stalks and dead flowers are kept tidily to-gether, ready to be transported in one load to the compost heap.

Orange flowers are often difficult to deal with in furnishings or interior decorating schemes because they present problems of colour, shade and tone. Marigolds and nasturtiums are obvious examples and although these are excellent flowers in their own way, they are sometimes unsympathetic in colour when asked to co-operate with softer tones. But a few marigolds combined with either pale yellow daisies from the border, the creamy white of meadow-sweet from a country hedgerow, a few short sprays of fennel or cream-white sweet peas will become much softer in tone while retaining the brightness of their original colour.

A bright splash of early autumn colouring is provided here by marigolds and fennel

However great the charm of a delicate flower arrangement, there are occasions when a splash of colour is indicated. Constance Spry used to say that there was great pleasure in occasionally having a group of what she described as 'clashing reds', though this comment came from a woman especially sensitive to soft colour effects – many of her own favourite arrangements were of the soft-toned old roses such as Madame Pierre Oger in a white glass vase, or a dolphin porcelain vase holding a few silvery rose-pink Conrad Meyers.

A splash of colour in anything – gardens, dress materials, furnishing, wallpapers, flower arrangements – demands certain conditions. First, there must be solid concentration of colour; second, there must be light and shade; and third, the most interesting and outstanding effects are often produced by what are usually considered to be clashing colours.

It would be difficult, if not impossible, to achieve a dramatic effect without a concentration of that colour. Try, for instance, arranging a handful of coral border carnations with blue-grey eucalyptus leaves. The foliage and stems of the carnations would blend with the eucalyptus and the general effect would be coral against blue-grey. This makes for a most attractive colour scheme but not a dramatic result.

A dress in flowered chiffon, or curtains in muslin or voile, may produce an effect of brightness but, unless there is a solid depth to the fabric so that no light shines through, an intense colouring effect cannot be obtained; so, with flowers, the deepest colours must be close together to exclude the light and there must be no delicate leaves, such as summer jasmine or *Rosa hugonis* foliage.

There must always be light and shade, but light in this instance refers to the light and shade in colouring of the flowers and berries. Here again (as one often finds with arranging flowers) the principles of painting apply. However bright the colours, no radiant effect can be produced unless there is a variation in tone – unless, in fact, there are shadows as well as high spots of colour.

An outstanding example of this is Renoir's *Les Parapluies*. The general overall impression of colour is undoubtedly blue, but to produce this effect there are many other colours and tones in the painting, the darkest being almost aubergine and the palest the colours in an opal.

So often one finds that something not designed for holding flowers becomes a most attractive background to an arrangement. A cooking board, I think, has many possibilities. It gives first of all a plain solid base. The texture of wood provides a link with the fir-cones, moss and berries, and the simple lines of the square complement the flowing lines of the branches. Because the board is heavy and of adequate size it will uphold much taller branches than something more fragile.

No apologies are necessary for writing, whenever an opportunity

Sprays of cotoneaster and berberis with their cheerful coloured berries arranged on a board with bold begonia flowers towards the centre

arises, about the rose. There is always a great deal to learn about modern roses which add to their numbers year by year, or about the old roses which have been grown and loved in this country perhaps since the days of the Roman occupation and certainly appearing in the early history of the Church.

There are, of course, roses which need extra care and sheltered positions. Some of them flower profusely for a short period, others go on steadily throughout the summer. And, particularly relevant to flower arrangement, there are roses which are suitable for cutting, more long-lasting than others, sweetly scented, and some with exceptional foliage.

How often do visitors to one's garden notice sweet-scented plants? People usually seem to be interested in colour, in water planting or in a piece of well-cut grass – and some are certainly enraptured by the more obvious sweet-smelling honeysuckle or lavender – but it is not my usual experience to find them especially looking out for scent.

As with perfume for the bath, for soap or toilet water, it is often the more subtle scent which is the most attractive, and so it usually is with flowers and leaves. The best scents amongst roses are often 'sweet but gentle'. Céleste, Madame Pierre Oger, Honorine de Brabant, Stanwell Perpetual and Gloire de Dijon, to mention only a few, have their own individual scent so that if one were blindfolded it might be possible to tell one from another after taking a deep sniff into the flower. Each of these very beautiful roses probably looks its best when two or three are arranged in a small vase and the scent is not mixed with other flowers.

Here are some ideas for using simple material in small arrangements.

A mixed group of early summer flowers, sweet rocket, mock orange (philadelphus), elder flower, columbine, lungwort foliage and various grasses: this little collection of rather soft and very simple flowers conveys a feeling of summer days as effectively as would more sophisticated material.

White viburnum flowers cut short with wedding grass (moraea) in a simple wicker basket painted dark green: green and white makes a fresh colour scheme, and the graceful, spear-like shape of the wedding grass, combined with its colouring, makes it a most useful addition to a flower arrangement.

A few roses in a porcelain basket: if some of the rose foliage can be spared from the bush, there is usually nothing better for showing off an almost fully blown rose. To be more effective some of the flowers should be cut much shorter than others and placed well down towards the centre, to show their full face.

A single rose with its own foliage, either in a tall, early champagne glass or an old scent bottle: a tall branch of a climbing rose can be arranged in a dark green, well-shaped wine bottle (especially attractive if a yellow rose such as Emily Gray or Gloire de Dijon is used).

Queen Anne's lace could be cut short with geums and lambs' ears (*Stachys lanata*) arranged in a low bread basket.

Two Gloire de Dijon roses in a small blue-grey glass jar

Peonies, two or three, or only one with either their own most attractive leaves or two or three sprays of mock orange (philadelphus) in flower, Chilean gum box (escallonia) or Japanese quince, depending on the colour of the peonies.

Foliage of iris and sprays of masterwort (astrantia) cut quite short, with their own leaves: the masterwort contrasts well with the iris spears.

Columbines (preferably yellow) with Queen Anne's lace, cut short, in an early sauce or gravy boat.

Clematis, two or three flowers with their curving stems and tendrils, arranged either on a flat dish for a table decoration, or in a decanter to show off the stems and leaves.

Geranium or pelargonium: green leaves banded with white (perhaps Dolly Varden), just a few short sprays arranged with white pinks cut short in a piece of white porcelain – a figurine or a white basket.

Ox-eye daisies in a small wicker basket, with Queen Anne's lace cut short and buttercups.

Mignonette arranged with the dark silver-grey foliage of *Convolvulus cneorum* and some of the lighter grey of *Helichrysum splendidum* and love-in-a-mist, all cut quite short and arranged rather in posy style in a small jug or container.

When you are doing the flowers for the house, do you first take a

A group of mixed dahlias are arranged
here against the large leaves of purple
cabbage, the flowers picking up the tones
and shades of the leaves which are
especially beautiful at this time of year

look at the room where they are going to be and decide their position, the right container, and the colours of flowers most attractive for the furnishings? Or do you go and see what there is in the garden or in the florist's window, choose the flowers, arrange them in the first container you find empty and then walk into the room wondering where they will look best?

There is something to be said for both these methods. But it seems clear that the position in the room should be chosen before anything else. On this depends the appropriate size of the arrangement, and if you are anywhere near a window the hardiness and condition of the flowers.

Flowers close to a window must (as for the hall) be reasonably impervious to draughts. Perhaps this may not apply in the depths of winter when one can be forgiven for keeping the windows securely shut. But if there is a bright, sunny morning and the window is opened, the flowers may not only be in a draught from the cold outside, but also may have to contend with the warmth of sunlight coming through the pane.

Apart from choosing flowers that will stand up to a draught, I have a preference for something that is in season. This is one of the rules of the Japanese school of flower arrangement. The Japanese are not allowed to arrange flowers that are out of their true season, which means there is more appreciation of a variety of material that might not otherwise become familiar.

The scope of flower arrangement is enlarged, as well as one's knowledge of plants – which often leads to greater interest. Certain beautiful flower blooms, such as gladioli and chrysanthemums for example, are splendid in their way but would be appreciated even more, I think, if they were used with some restraint and not throughout the year.

Having decided the position in the room, the suitability of a container and the best flowers and foliage available, one comes to the practical side of the arrangement. It seems to me that great value can come from doing the flowers in position and I want to emphasize this very strongly. One argument against it is that when the room is polished and dusted it will be difficult not to leave traces of working on the spot; small bits of leaves and stalks would at once give the impression of untidiness, especially if the floor has just been polished.

However, it is possible to leave the room exactly as you found it if you spread newspapers or, as I mentioned earlier, a dustsheet. A duster or papers can be laid on the surface of the furniture where the arrangement is going to stand and a large dustsheet should cover the floor space below.

I think it is easier by this method to get the arrangement into better perspective with its surroundings, and to achieve a harmonious shape and outline. If the group is wide and spreading, with branches at interesting angles, arranging it in position eliminates the risk of these branches being knocked or broken when carried through doorways.

Fuchsias in a shallow white bowl

128

It also means that the group will be arranged at the correct level.

The proportion, or scale, of tower and steeple to the body of a church, of furniture to the dimensions of a room, or of trees to the surrounding garden, are just a few examples which show that, to be harmonious, objects must relate in size to one another.

Flowers are no exception. As a study of painting can be most helpful in learning about the use of colour, so the study of proportion in architecture, sculpture and design of porcelain and furnishings can give valuable guidance in flower arrangement. This does not mean being highly technical with a tape measure or set-square, but one can try to train the eye so that the right or wrong proportion is immediately apparent.

A sense of scale is something the Japanese have acquired: 'In their gardens, as in their architecture, in the arrangement of flowers, as in their dress, the minimum is expressed and the maximum left for the beholder to supply.' Using only a little material or a small vase is not necessarily the implication here but, rather, applying a certain restraint. Scale is important when growing flowers for cutting. Outsize blooms are often just as incongruous in the border as in the house. For example, how much more clumsy on their thin stems and overbearing to their delicate foliage are the large trusses of some new sweet peas compared with the beautifully shaped smaller clusters of the older varieties, which are in perfect proportion to the tracery of the stems, tendrils and leaves.

The question of scale is an important factor in this arrangement based on a still life by Balthasar van der Ast, in the use of shells and the blue vase with Stanwell Perpetual roses and carnations. In this sophisticated form of art, flowers are carefully related in colour, texture and size to other natural objects: fruit, insects, wood, stone, fabric, wine and food.

The scale of the accessories in any still life painting must be in the right proportions to the whole, as can be learnt from the Dutch school, from Chardin and many painters of today.

In this still life the small shells are just as important as the larger ones and the round dark chestnuts, almost the smallest objects in the whole picture, not only echo the colour of the vine leaves and the darker tones of two shells but also, by their size, take their right place in the balance of the painting.

In the same way the roses with their delicate leaves and tight cream buds are in proportion to the size and shape of the blue Chinese vase. Roses that are more flamboyant – such as Rosa Mundi – would be out of scale not only with the vase but with other components of the group.

The Stanwell Perpetual rose is one of the finest of the Scots briar roses and one that is really 'perpetual'. It has double soft blush-pink flowers, sometimes 15 to 18 cm (2 to 3 in) across, with a sweet scent, which come out during summer and then, after a short rest, come on again at a time when they are most welcome – that is, in the autumn.

The great pleasure two or three of these roses can give in a glass and the delight of the subtle perfume in the room, can only be discovered by growing them. They are very lovely.

The foliage has the usual lightness and charm of the Scots briar roses and the shrub sends out long shoots which produce the background for a tall, sturdy bush. There are also many curving branches and when the pale pink buds are coming out between the rather fragile leaves, the effect is entrancing.

Balthasar van der Ast was much influenced by the early flower painter Jan Brueghel and his work dates from about the end of the sixteenth century until the middle of the seventeenth. It is interesting to notice the foundations of probably the greatest school of flower painting throughout the centuries and to realize that it sprang from impecunious beginnings. So much so that the story goes that the fees given to artists for their paintings were so small that on one occasion a poor peasant woman asked Brueghel to paint for her a bunch of flowers which she could not afford to buy, which gives some idea of the state of poverty of the painter before he became recognized.

Stanwell Perpetual roses and three border carnations provide the only fresh flowers in this copy of a still life painting. The components of the picture are selected to give an example of the care and thought expended on the various small details included in such a painting

The brightness of viburnum berries contrasts here with purple sea lavender, honeysuckle and wild clematis in this basket arrangement

There is a simple charm in the paintings of van der Ast, showing clearly a love and respect for the separate flowers and leaves and affection for the smallest shells and other details.

Honeysuckle, *Clematis vitalba*, scarlet berries, wild seedheads and a clump of lilac-coloured sea lavender – these were the findings of two recent country walks, one close to the sea and the other some miles inland.

Let us talk about the different plants one by one.

Known perhaps more for its fluffy seedheads than for the charm of its delicate cream-white flowers, *Clematis vitalba* is our native species, known more familiarly as traveller's joy, the name first given to it by Gerard in the 16th century. It has had various uses since that time: its tough stems were good for binding faggots and short lengths were sometimes cut by countrymen and smoked, hence the names gypsies' bacca and smoking cane. But the plant was never used medicinally as its leaves are poisonous.

Another hedgerow plant which gives curving outlines for flower arrangement is honeysuckle. Cut when still in bud it will last quite well, despite a frequent criticism that it is not long-lasting. Its soft cream-white-yellow colouring is especially delicate in tone and combines well with other flowers, such as mignonette or Madame Pierre Oger roses. It also looks most attractive with certain grey-foliaged plants such as the curry plant (*Helichrysum angustifolium*) or *H. splendidum*. Sometimes it shows to best advantage when arranged alone.

The sweet scent of honeysuckle should be given a chance to pervade the room unchallenged, so it is important not to put it into a vase with other heavily scented flowers such as nasturtiums, *Salvia turkestanica* (although the colouring is good with this) or pinks. Honeysuckle is easy to grow under almost any conditions, whether in a small space in a town garden, perhaps in a north-facing corner, or in a tub. It can also be used for an arbour where shade or shelter from the wind is needed. In such conditions, the full benefit of its scent can be appreciated.

Berries abound in most hedgerows. Two common and lovely flowering shrubs, the guelder rose (*Viburnum opulus*) and the wayfaring tree (*V. lantana*) belong to the same family.

The last contribution to this collection is sea lavender (limonium) which happens to have come from a country walk taken close to the sea. For anyone interested in wild flowers by the sea there is a reliable guide: *Flowers of the Coast* by Ian Hepburn (Collins) in which there is a colour illustration of sea lavender growing in a Suffolk saltmarsh, exactly where my bunch came from. Those wishing for something not too technical might be encouraged by the dedication of this book: 'To Phyllis who loves the sea but is sometimes uncertain of her botany'.

Sea lavender, with its thin stems and soft colouring, may seem rather anaemic in effect when taken piece by piece. But seen at a

A bunch of zinnias in various colours in a blue bulb vase

distance the cumulative impression of its growth and colouring is like a sheet of amethyst lying among the reeds and rushes. The same thing applies when it is used in arrangements: a tight clump will give a more definite feeling of colour than the same number of stems spread out among other material.

Arranging flowers to emphasize a furnishing scheme, to contrast with or repeat the tones of accessories, is a useful exercise but, sometimes, why not just have colour because it is irresistible: either a bright splash, or the subtle shades frequently found in a painting by Chardin? Both colour ranges can be found in an autumn garden, on one of those days of 'mists and mellow fruitfulness' which make this season so beautiful.

Bring this colour into the house, either in tones of foliage with, for instance, *Parrotia persica*, maple, *Magnolia grandiflora*, *Ginkgo biloba*, berberis; or in nasturtiums, snapdragons, marigolds, nemesias and zinnias.

Softly glowing zinnias remind one of the colours of semi-precious stones: topaz, amethyst and agate, with here and there brilliant orange and red, intense against the white paint and china in the photograph above.

There are many varieties: State Fair – giant flowered, in colours of salmon, rose, orange, purple, lavender, yellow and scarlet. Merry-go-Round – these zinnias have quilled petals with tips in a different colouring from the rest of the petals. They come in many colours.

Peppermint – these are medium-sized flowers, striped in red and yellow, pink and white, orange and yellow or purple and white.

Zinnia haageana is a dwarf bushy species with semi-double or single flowers in various colours.

Apart from the outline, light and shade are probably regarded as the two most important factors to consider in a water colour or oil painting. Sometimes in furnishings or flower arrangements this is a point which may be overlooked and, as a result, there is a monotony in the effect.

In the photograph below these factors are dealt with by contrasting pale foliage with the darker tones of autumn flowers, but change of tone is not the only way in which to create an arrangement of light and shade. Sometimes a light effect is achieved almost as much by shape and texture as by colour.

The solid shape of the dark red flower heads of the *Sedum spectabile* are arranged with *Phlomis fruticosa* foliage. Although the leaves are delicate in shape and light in colour, their velvety texture gives them a solidity that needs to be well lit, or the whole effect would be that of shade.

Having created such a flower arrangement based on the idea of light and shade, this effect can be intensified, as we have done, by placing the vase under direct lighting. At this time of year when we close our curtains earlier and turn on the lights a display such as this will become a lively and dramatic focal point in the room.

If given special consideration, and planted in a sheltered position against a south wall in a light sandy soil, phlomis will develop into

Grey phlomis leaves and sedum flowers

a taller shrub with bigger flowers after three or four years. It is outstandingly attractive as a garden plant when grown in this way, with its panicles of buttercup-yellow flowers growing up the stem in candelabra style.

Many people do not yet realize the comparative hardiness of some of these grey-foliaged plants and feel that they are not worth troubling about if they will not come through the winter. But it is surprising how hardy some of them are and how well they stand up to quite severe frosts and, almost worse, biting winds. I find that they like the protection of other plants growing quite close to them and, although they may look rather bedraggled during the coldest months, they soon recover when the warmer weather comes. From the point of view of flower arrangement they are invaluable.

Perhaps the best known of all the grey-leaved plants is *Senecio laxifolius* or garden ragwort. This is one of the plants which can literally be killed by kindness. It prefers rather rough conditions, growing well at the top of a low wall in soil which has a certain amount of rubble in it. Once established it will probably double its size in a year, and sends out clusters of soft grey-white buds at the beginning of June which will later open out into daisy-like yellow flowers. The rather flat, lobe-like leaves are greeny-grey on the front with an almost startling white on the reverse side. They thus provide opportunities for use with dramatic effects and colour schemes, and as they are available throughout the winter as well as the summer months they are valuable indeed. The leaves are also useful for dried arrangements (they may be pressed between sheets of newspaper under a heavy weight), giving a rare gleam of white which is often difficult to find in other plant material.

In the photograph the silver-grey leaves with serrated edges, rather like old lace, come from the plant *Senecio cineraria*, another member of the senecio family. There is ample opportunity for using this attractive foliage with many different flowers but it may be well to remember that it tends to look too opulent if used in large quantities. Like some of the other showy plants which are connected in our minds with Victorian bedding-out schemes, a little goes a long way. But this is not the fault of the plant, which in itself is graceful and most decorative. It is the inartistic use which has sometimes been made of it that has diminished its value.

The third grey-leaved plant I want to emphasize is the rather spiky one with thin, branchlike stems. Its official name is *Helichrysum splendidum*, and it has an elegant manner of growth. The small branches spread into interesting shapes and the leaves grow well down the stem. This plant should be given some protection from winter weather and then it will come through most cold spells. Its shape is useful for many flower arrangements and, as shown here, with berries. It combines equally well with strong colours and also with softer shades such as cyclamen or anemones. It will last well in an arrangement for at least a fortnight.

The sparkling berries of the Kiftsgate rose and its tawny leaves provide a contrast for the silver-grey, almost lacelike foliage of *Senecio cineraria*

The berries and the grey foliage are arranged in a solid pewter jar and anchored in large-mesh wire netting. They should make a long-lasting group.

The Kiftsgate rose has attractive clusters of berries, elegant in shape and in the arrangement of their thin stems and especially interesting in colouring. The few russet leaves are some of those still left on the rose stems and come in shades which merge to perfection with the clear, almost scarlet colour of the berries. Everything about this rose is light, delicate and almost fragile looking for cutting at this stage. However, it is far from fragile, growing to enormous heights as it does on strong, stout branches. Nevertheless, for a foliage arrangement in the autumn, the whole style and colouring of the berries and leaves is unique and of great value.

The lacelike silver-grey foliage of *Senecio cineraria* carries on this feeling of lightness both in tone and texture and, although the colouring and container are the same as that in the photograph on p. 135, the feeling of the one group is firm and solid and could not be more different from the other. There are, of course, other roses with scarlet hips – amongst them some of the Penzance briars and the Wolley Dod's rose – but it would be difficult to find, I think, anything more delicate and graceful than these rather small hips in groupings on thin stems. Certainly their colour is unusual with its slightly orange tint and shows up especially well against silver grey.

Winter Arrangements

Why should contrast in colour and shape be so important in a large foliage group? Anyone with limited garden space or with virtually only a closed yard will know the answer. When plants and evergreens are amongst paving, standing in a tub or climbing up a basement wall, it is essential to make a selection of plants which suit the background and show up against each other.

This same principle also applies to flower arrangement: in such a collection of leaves, all of varying textures, colours and shapes, it is possible to get many different effects.

On the left of the picture is honey-coloured wild maple from the hedgerows aginst black privet berries, wine-coloured *Viburnum fragrans* foliage and silver-grey-green *Senecio laxifolius* (garden ragwort). Golden privet or the turning foliage of the rose Blanc Double de Coubert could be substituted for maple.

Near the hydrangea leaves towards the centre is a cluster of *Senecio cineraria*, with a spray of laurustinus in flower and a few small stems of *Helichrysum splendidum*. To the left of the leaves are snowberry tree, spindle, black privet berries and a tall branch of dark green cistus. So there is already a variety of contrasts.

The texture is also valuable, for example, the ribbed effect of veining on the *Viburnum fragrans* leaves, the velvety senecios and the shining smoothness of the privet berries.

At the top centre is a branch of *Cotoneaster horizontalis* with forsythia foliage, varying from quite a bright green to soft yellow, the thin effect of broom, bright red rose hips and a tall spray of rosemary set off by the coppery *Parrotia persica*. (Turning beech foliage could also provide this colouring.)

Next comes the *Fatsia japonica* leaf, emphasized by a cluster of rose hips. This is one of the most reliable shrubs for the smallest garden and does just as well in a pot. The shrub prefers a sheltered, but not necessarily sunny, position, with a little extra cosseting through winter until it is well established.

To the right of the group is the contrast of a large, fanlike globe artichoke with the rich brown dried head. Beside the globe artichoke is a clump of *Phlomis fruticosa* (Jerusalem sage), sturdy and long-lasting when cut. There are stems of variegated periwinkle with curving sprays and heart-shaped leaves; and a few grasses, branches of

A collection of winter foliage which includes rosemary, globe artichoke, cistus, phlomis and laurustinus with berries of privet, cotoneaster and some rose hips

vine and azalea, with the sunshine colouring of golden privet.

Miss Sackville-West wrote of 'finding something to pick for indoors' in winter months: 'A flowerless room is a soul-less room, to my thinking; but even one solitary little vase of a living flower may redeem it'.

It seems to me that the two most obvious solutions are the use of foliage and/or chrysanthemums, and dried flower arrangements. The important thing is to have as large a selection of material as possible in your garden, using evergreens, a few flowers, early branches of fruit trees, berries, pressed or preserved leaves, together with a few house plants which can also be useful for cutting. It is often just a question of making the most use of a small space.

Periwinkle, with its shining dark or variegated leaves, will grow on most shaded banks, and the dramatic Christmas and Lenten roses will produce their magnificent foliage almost all the year round, demanding only a cool place for their roots and not too much sun on the bed. Then there is variegated holly, with a dark leaf like laurel or camellia – a wonderful contrast. Golden privet is another possibility for most of the year and Portugal laurel has branches of beautifully pointed dark leaves.

Rosemary and garden ragwort (*Senecio laxifolius*) go bravely into the frosty weather; so do *Garrya elliptica* with its grey-green catkins, and *Pieris japonica* whose leaves grow in fan-like clusters with racemes of white flowers. These will add interest and give variety of shapes and colours. Also useful are bergenia and bay.

In the shops one can buy eucalyptus, and silkbark oak (grevillea), branches of pussy willow, bunches of pittosporum, laurel, yew and box. The two most important things to remember about this particular material are that the base of the branches must be split open or smashed to allow a greater intake of water, and the water supply must be kept up well.

Rosemary seems to me to be an essential plant to have, however small the garden. I think I would grow it in a tub if there was no other space. Its cheerful habit and regular, energetic growth, its leaves of dark green backed with light grey and its clouds of blue-grey flowers in April and May – these are some of its attractions. Another, and perhaps the most important, is its scent.

Rosmarinus (dew-of-the-sea) grows naturally near the sea but thrives and flourishes in inland gardens. Probably first introduced into this country by the Romans, it was always one of the treasured plants in the herb gardens of the monasteries and the kitchen gardens of Elizabethan days. A Spanish legend says that rosemary flowers were originally white, but during the flight into Egypt the Holy Family rested beside a rosemary bush. The Virgin Mary threw her robe over it and the flowers took on its blue colouring in honour of her memory.

Anne of Cleves, arriving at Greenwich as a bride, wore 'on her head a coronet of gold and precious stones, set full of branches of

A small group of white chrysanthemums with bergenia leaves and *Rosa hugonis* foliage, illustrating the importance of placing a flower arrangement close to a light on winter evenings

rosemary'. Regarded as a royal flower it also stood for friendship. Sir Thomas More wrote: 'As for rosemary, I lette it runne all over my garden walls, not onlie because my bees love it, but because it is the herb sacred to remembrance and friendship, whence a sprig of it hath a dumb language'.

It lasts for weeks when cut for the house and gives a faint elusive perfume of great charm.

Camellia foliage, glistening and green – could there be a better colour of green? Camellias may be seen almost everywhere in the British Isles – at The Royal Horticultural Society's gardens at Wisley, at Kew, in the Savill Gardens at Windsor, at Bodnant in Wales where they are a speciality, at Annesgrove in County Cork, at Nymans in Sussex where they are widely represented and grow superbly, and in many of the other National Trust gardens, especially in Cornwall, Somerset and Scotland.

Camellia japonica was being cultivated in this country as long ago as 1739 and was the first member of the genus to be introduced into Europe.

Chrysanthemums – mentioned specifically at the beginning of this list of suggestions for winter vases – are a standby at this time of the year. The garden ones will be finished now and most of those in the shops will have been produced with a certain amount of heat. The Wisley chrysanthemum trials seem to provide new plants each year in

Another example of lighting a small group, in this case branches of winter jasmine with the beautiful foliage of *Nandina domestica*. This plant bears leaves throughout the year in a variety of shades which are unusual and always decorative

bewildering quantity and so a visit to Wisley might help one to make a selection of plants best suited to cutting. The Korean chrysanthemums will withstand five to ten degrees of frost without damage to the new buds, giving a continuous display well into the winter months. But most plant catalogues will list the latest tested plants.

This family provides some of the best-lasting, most reliable of all flowers for arrangement. The order includes greenhouse varieties but it also embraces hardy perennials, annuals and shrubby plants. All those mentioned are easily grown in any good garden soil.

The name chrysanthemum derives from two Greek words, *chrysos* meaning golden and *anthemon* meaning flower. All chrysanthemums are not necessarily golden – some types are white, and in the florist's chrysanthemums there is a wide colour range, but it seems that this must have been the original colour.

These flowers appear in late summer and early in the autumn and go on until November. They should be watered freely in the summer and given liquid manure from July to September. They are available in a wide colour range and it might be helpful to consult a specialist's catalogue.

To return to foliage: the wall spotlight shows up the delicate outline of *Nandina domestica* foliage arranged in a glass bottle with winter jasmine. *Nandina domestica* (akin to berberis) is sometimes known as the Chinese sacred bamboo; the Chinese plant it near their houses for good luck. In this country it prefers a sunny, well-sheltered position.

As it was through Miss Jekyll's reference to this plant that I first knew it, I should like to quote from her description of it. Referring to the Chinese belief in its bringing of good fortune she writes in *Wood and Garden*:

'If it is as lucky as it is pretty, it ought to do one good! I first made acquaintance with this beautiful plant in Canon Ellacombe's most interesting garden at Bitton, in Gloucestershire, where it struck me as one of the most beautiful growing things I had ever seen, the beauty being mostly in the form and colouring of the leaves. It is not perhaps a plant for everybody, and barely hardy; it seems slow to get hold, and its full beauty only shows when it is well established, and throws up its wonderfully coloured leaves on tall bamboo-like stalks.'

One thing is common to these two arrangements and that is they stand close to or under a lamp. This point has already been mentioned but it is almost an essential one here. Flowers in winter time need as much lighting as possible in order to show up anything particularly delicate such as the formation of leaves in the *Nandina domestica*. It is grown frequently in hot countries – in quantities in the south of France, for example, and it is often dried up by the time that winter comes after all the hot sun of summer. But it retains its leaves, usually at this time in quite a regular green, and these need light of some kind to show their beautiful shape.

Perhaps these photographs and plant lists may help to show how

Using a wall bracket. Leaves of *Senecio cineraria* with hips of the Kiftsgate rose

it is possible to have simple flower or foliage decorations from the garden during this time.

As Mr Jason Hill remarked in a chapter headed 'Something to Look at in Winter': 'It may often be wise to tell expectant visitors that there is nothing to see in the garden, but we need never, I think, say it to ourselves.' (*The Contemplative Gardener*. Faber & Faber, 1940.)

Perhaps almost as much as pedestals, wall brackets have played a significant part in the development of flower decoration in this country during the last two hundred years. The Leeds factory made some of the first brackets as early as 1745 and from Staffordshire others came a decade or so later. But wall brackets do not by any means have to be either of pottery or porcelain. They can be made of wire, of copper, of basket weave, silver or wrought ironwork, and they can also take the form of a console table fixed to the wall in the manner of a bracket.

There are many advantages to be obtained from using wall brackets. Economy is one of them. It is often possible, at a difficult time of the year when flowers may be scarce and expensive, to do an arrangement in a wall bracket using very little material. I have a friend who has converted a large old-fashioned tureen lid into a bracket by having it cut lengthways in half. In this, depending on what material she has to hand, she can either stand a jam jar or two, which will take spreading branches, or else she uses pot plants.

A wall bracket can give extra emphasis to a colour scheme or help to furnish a difficult area of wall. The wall space need not necessarily be large – sometimes the space between two windows will take a narrow bracket quite comfortably or a small, upright arrangement could look effective under wall lights.

The fact that a bracket is up on a wall out of the way and at a reasonable height can be of great value for decorations for public functions. Often there is no suitable piece of furniture to take a vase, and nothing of enough height to show such an arrangement of flowers. This applies especially to a marquee, where brackets can be attached to the marquee poles. It is also a useful way of displaying flowers out of the way of small children.

Large areas of bare walls may be made more attractive by the use of wall brackets placed in strategic positions. I remember such a situation where simple metal brackets had been used at intervals up the walls of a tall staircase, painted the same colour and holding pots of ivy pelargoniums and trailing ivy. When the trails became long enough they were linked up with the next bracket higher or lower down the staircase and the effect was almost like an indoor winter garden.

Wall brackets can also be of value in a garden room or conservatory. In this context plants such as tradescantias, variegated periwinkle, ivy, pelargoniums etc. would probably be more in keeping than flowers. Material to be used in wall brackets can either be fresh flowers, foliage, dried flowers or leaves, or pot plants, according to the time of year or the effect required. A wall bracket containing bare branches can be most effective against a plain, light-coloured wall, if a 'line' effect is required.

Church decorations sometimes demand flowers in difficult positions, and one of the most awkward is the decoration of pillars, the pulpit or sloping windowsills. A bracket can be most useful in such cases.

The photographs on pages 144 and 147 show berries and leaves in a metal wall bracket and dried flowers in a porcelain one. The background is obviously of the greatest importance to show off the material and in both cases it is plain.

Water is a problem in most wall brackets and the level must be watched carefully. In porcelain ones a hole is sometimes made rather low down at the back for hanging on a nail and this unfortunately reduces the amount of water it will hold. Anchorage is of some importance and can vary considerably, depending on the size and type of the bracket.

The collecting, pressing and drying of leaves and flowers is often connected with mid-Victorian times. After all, this was when young ladies were encouraged by their governesses to go on flower-collecting expeditions in the country lanes; the assembling of the flowers promoted botanical instruction and the arranging of them often formed a useful wet-day occupation.

However, there were experiments in drying flowers as early as the 16th century. Sir Hugh Platt, a courtier in the reign of Elizabeth I, described such an experiment in his small book *Delights for Ladies*. According to his instructions, roses, carnations and marigolds should be cut on a dry day and then laid flat on a layer of sand in small shallow boxes. They should be covered by more sand, taking care that the flowers are kept as flat as possible and in their natural shape. These boxes should then be placed in 'some warme sunny place'.

I have tried this experiment, putting the flowers into wooden boxes in a cool oven, and the result was most exciting. They emerged in good shape and colour, but I found one big disadvantage: it is only possible to do a limited number at a time.

Apart from this rather specialized application of dried flowers there have been only a few instances of their use for decoration until the post-war years. There are, however, isolated references by Gertrude Jekyll and Mrs Earle. Miss Jekyll writing in 1900 remarks of the *Eryngium giganteum* that it 'is a handsome object if kept dry, lasting well for several months, and losing but little of its form and lustre'.

Mrs Earle in her book *Pot Pourri from a Surrey Garden* writes of having 'two bright green olive jars into which are stuck large bunches of the white seed vessels of honesty and some flowers of everlastings (*Helichrysum bracteatum*)'. But it is only recently that their uses have been realized as an answer to central heating conditions.

There are many different flowers and seedheads from the herbaceous border and wild hedgerow plants which have been found to dry successfully. Perhaps we might start with Miss Jekyll's *Eryngium giganteum*, a relative of the sea holly.

The eryngium is illustrated in the photograph, and makes a useful foundation for many colour schemes. Here it is mixed in with other shades, but it also combines well with the deep brown and russet of sorrel and dock, or it will form a useful contrast to the yellow of achillea and to *Alchemilla mollis*.

The white seed pods of honesty, mentioned by Mrs Earle, are well known, and they can also look most attractive if the grey-brown outer cases are not peeled off. Again, if they are dried when still in their green state they can be invaluable.

It is in the everlastings that the false colouring of dried flowers is likely to be seen. 'There has been invented also a method of tinting the lily, thanks to the taste of mankind for monstrous productions,' wrote Pliny in his *Natural History* in AD 77. Unfortunately this applies just as much today. It is quite unnecessary to colour, dye, or

Dried flowers and seedheads in a porcelain wall bracket. These include the flowers of globe artichoke, hop, anaphalis and seedheads of spiraea, iris, columbine, delphinium, love-in-a-mist, nipplewort, dock and phlomis

stain dried flowers in any way; they are much more beautiful in their own soft colours.

Although the natural colours of dried flowers are usually soft it is possible to get a good deal of variety. The predominating colour of most seedheads is probably brown, but the many shades of brown range from the soft pale buff of nipplewort, through the coppers and burnt siennas of dock and iris seedheads to the deep vandyke brown of globe artichokes.

An example of an arrangement in shades of blue comes with a small amount of contrasting yellow. Larkspur will afford deep purple, pale pink and white; acanthus gives a grey-white, with a deep purple tinge; and hydrangeas produce pinky-brown, aubergine and sometimes lime green.

The most usual method of drying is that of hanging the flowers and seedheads upside down in bunches in a dry atmosphere. A cool airing cupboard is a good, general choice, or a dry, sunny attic, or a very cool greenhouse is also suitable. I have seen bunches of delphiniums being dried on an upstairs landing.

Certainly the material must be in good condition when cut, and should also be dry, but other variations of temperature, the coolness or heat of the day when it is cut, as well as the outside temperature when it is drying, make it difficult to lay down hard and fast rules. I have also found that material which had dried quite well one year has failed another for no accountable reason. But this is half the fun of drying flowers and almost anything can be tried.

Here are some suggestions for materials for colour schemes:
Dark brown and off-white. Off-white nigella seedheads, anaphalis and iris seedheads.

A table decoration of dried flowers and seedheads under a lamp. The light will show up the shapes of the seedheads and flowers but should not be too bright, otherwise it will take the colour from them

Blue, yellow, grey and white. Honesty, delphinium, anaphalis, barley, poppy heads, alliums, hydrangea, *Stachys lanata* and sea lavender.

Grey and rich copper-brown. Branches of deep brown sorrel and dock, with pearl-grey alliums cut to different heights. This can be varied by adding white larkspur.

Brown, grey and blue. Tall stems of acanthus flowers with alliums, delphiniums, sweet rocket and water plantain; with globe thistle, eryngium, globe artichokes, anaphalis and *Stachys lanata*.

Green, brown and scarlet. Amaranthus, greater plantain, poppy heads, globe artichokes, iris seedheads, nigella, *Iris foetidissima*.

Ochre yellow and pale green. Yellow achillea with branches of hop flowers or lime seedheads, following the line of the achilleas.

Brown, grey, off-white and soft blue. Sea lavender, alliums, sea holly, corn, giant reed, hare's-tail grass, teasels, reed mace, bur-reed.

Mixed colours. Wheat, grasses, quake-grass, gypsophila cut very short, *Helichrysum bracteatum*, globe thistle, white and yellow gnaphalium.

Dark brown, light tan and grey. Magnolia leaves, dark teasels and pale poppy heads.

Dark brown and purple-grey. Globe artichoke heads with iris seed pods, sea lavender and purple larkspur.

The texture of the container is of the greatest importance. Wirework and basketware are materials which always seem to combine most successfully with a dried arrangement and of the two a basket is the easier to arrange. There is something soft and pliable and yielding about a basket and it provides a base into which the stems of dried flowers can be easily fixed so that they are held in position firmly and steadily.

The dried flower group in the photograph has to stand up to direct overhead lighting – the kind frequently used for a dining table. This means that everything in it must be in first-class condition, revealing the contrast in shape of the individual seedheads quite as much as the colour. These are arranged on the wooden lid of a large French cheese-box, the stems being fixed into a wedge of brown plasticine. The three globe artichoke heads are each in different stages of development and the central one has taken on almost the quality of carved wood. These provide the chief features of the group, most of the other material acting as a framework for them.

The almost yellow ochre colouring of the *Alchemilla mollis* seems quite bright when contrasted with the natural buff shades of eryngium or sea holly. (Sometimes this plant retains a steel-blue colouring, especially in the stems.) The rather nut-brown tones of the iris seedheads are echoed by the rounded *Phlomis fruticosa* and by the seeds of *Hosta sieboldiana*, although the seed cases are much lighter. Contrast both in shape and texture comes with the clusters of *Anaphalis triplinervis* and towards the centre are stems of the thread-like grey-white curry plant.

Fundamentals

Before the latter half of the 18th century, vases were regarded in England as attractive ornaments and were not specifically intended for flower displays. Then the Wedgwood bough-pots and the Leeds factory's wall brackets appeared, evidence that arrangements of flowers and branches were being introduced for decorative effect, and needing purpose-designed containers.

The wide selection of vases we have today is the result of nearly 200 years of evolution in the creation of new shapes and the reproduction of old ones. Which are the most attractive, suitable and widely used containers? It is an interesting question to consider when looking through a collection of vases, searching for the right one for a large-scale table arrangement or to hold just a few roses.

One certain fact emerges: the usefulness of a pedestal. I do not refer to a tall column supporting a large vase for church decoration, but just a small, sometimes very slight one to give extra height. Containers which achieve this height may be baskets, candlesticks, sauceboats, teapots, wine glasses, decanters and porcelain dessert dishes or cake-stands such as the one illustrated here.

It is thought to be an early 19th-century product of the Rockingham factory, and is almost perfect for flowers. It not only has a slender pedestal with a firm, rounded base, but a bowl-shaped top with handles, deep enough to hold plenty of water. In many cases such a design is almost flat and an extra container for water, for example a shallow sandwich baking tin, is needed. This makes an upright arrangement more difficult to achieve, although a tall wedge of Oasis standing firmly in wire netting, and the use of funnels, would be helpful.

This might be worth while for a special occasion, but a shallow tin is capable of providing a base for a spreading arrangement without extra contrivances if flowers are cut short towards the centre. This is a shape especially suitable for buffet decorations, when the group is seen from above, so that it should be fairly low and spreading without straggling.

The flowers in the photograph are arranged in crumpled large-mesh wire netting, pulled down slightly at the sides where it is fixed through the handles for greater security. If branches are being arranged, a large, heavy pinholder might be more suitable for anchorage.

Although strictly perennials, petunias are grown as half-hardy annuals, and used as bedding-out plants. They will grow in almost any soil and are not fussy as to situation, although they prefer the sun. A great number of new varieties have been developed in recent years. Here are some of them:

Red Ensign has bright scarlet flowers and a dwarf habit; Blue Lustre has large, deep blue flowers; and then there are Pink, Red and Peach Satin, Blue Lagoon which is a deep violet-blue, Mercury, a light sky blue and Red Cap, supposed to be a deeper, brighter red than Red Satin. For a yellow petunia there is Brass Band Improved although it is not described as a true rich yellow.

Then there are the grandiflora petunias, especially recommended for window-boxes and tubs. First comes a yellow, Sunburst, the first yellow F_1 grandiflora, introduced in 1966. It is free-flowering, dwarf and spreading, and a good companion for Apple Blossom which has won the All-America Award. Other new grandiflora petunias include Dream Parade, crimson and white; Highlight, salmon; Velvet Queen, crimson-purple; Ace of Hearts, deep scarlet; and Candy Apple, which is a very bright scarlet. Then there is something which sounds like a strip of the rainbow called Bonanza Mixture, including about seven clear colours and described as a 'desirable novelty'. For gardening these bright colours can be useful in producing a cheerful effect with relatively little trouble – a certain amount of watering is entailed during a hot spell. But it is the white petunias which I have personally found to be most valuable.

For arrangement, petunias can help to provide any required colour at a time when it may not be available in other plants in the garden. Plants are usually available in May; seed may be sown under glass in early spring.

Overleaf: A basket arrangement or 'tussie-mussie' of flowers from the garden, which includes astrantia, anaphalis, phlox, hosta leaves, *Euonymus radicans* and the tall yellow panicles of senecio

This table arrangement of petunias is given height by a pedestal porcelain cake stand. This kind of container also encourages a spreading effect

Branches of lilac and bergenia show here the value of a well-shaped teapot as a container for flowers

A teapot may not appear, at first sight, to be suitable for flowers. The shape is unusual – quite different from any other type of container whether specifically used as a vase or not. The opening is nearly always small, which would seem to make it difficult to fit in many stems, especially thick ones.

This may appear to be a drawback but, in fact it turns out to be a distinct advantage, since the small space provides good anchorage for the flowers. There is generally no need for wire netting, pinholders, or Oasis, as the flowers will usually stay in position.

Owing to the depth of an average teapot and its capacity for holding three or four cups of tea, there is an ample supply of water for a quantity of flowers and in spite of the difficulty of fitting in thick stems there is unexpectedly plenty of room for branches – the lilac and bergenia in the photograph are proof of this. Neither of these have thin stems – far from it – but they both fit in together with plenty of space, a good deep supply of water, and are firmly anchored. A small amount of wire netting was used in this case to give support to the weight of the lilac branches.

The spout and handle of the teapot should be allowed to stand out and not be covered over with leaves or flowers. They are part of the design and as such they should be seen.

As with most vases, the shape of the teapot dictates the outline and size of the arrangement. This lustre teapot is unusually tall and so will take upright stems, but an oval-shaped Lowestoft design, or the round, chubby breakfast type of teapot, would suggest a more spreading shape.

Many people know the leaves of *Bergenia cordifolia*. In arrangement they are invaluable, coming in different sizes and colours from large, dark leathery ones to the fresh green, and slightly folded shape, of the new ones. It may be worth also mentioning *Bergenia crassifolia*, with wine-red leaves in winter.

Lilac is such an old friend – there can be few gardens without it – that its usefulness may sometimes be taken for granted. The best-known and the one common to most gardens is *Syringa vulgaris*, which has the usual 'lilac' colouring. The name lilac is derived from the Persian '*nilak*' meaning 'blueish', and so presumably this lilac colouring was the original one.

In the most informed botanical circles lilac is known as syringa, and looking back one finds a reason for this.

J. C. Loudon, writing in 1838, tells us that the blue and the white varieties were cultivated by Gerard and Parkinson in 1597 under the names of the blue-pipe and the white-pipe, and were confused with *Philadelphus coronarius* which was also called the old English pipe-tree. So this name applied to both lilac and philadelphus.

It seems, therefore, that in trying to remember to call a lilac a syringa we are only reverting to what our great-grandfathers must have called it. In many country districts, just to add to the confusion, it was often referred to as the 'laycock'.

Such a collection of material as that in the above photograph must be arranged in something which holds plenty of water, and a small pedestal effect helps to show off the various blooms so that they are seen to better advantage. Both these points are taken care of in this silver entree dish. The lid, upturned and holding the water, stands on the base of the dish which provides the extra height.

Perhaps the most unusual in colouring are the small-flowered tobacco plants (nicotianas). These are invaluable for their introduction of a soft lime green, probably not to be found in any other plant. This is an important, as well as an interesting colour, for it acts as a link between all the various tones in the arrangement.

Solidity is given to the group by the roundness of marigolds and zinnias. In both cases the harshness of the deep orange flowers is much softened by the pale yellow ones. This colour note is also repeated in the nemesias.

A touch of clear yellow comes from calceolaria – a little of this goes a long way, I think, but in small quantities it is a good colour. Sprays of honeysuckle bring contrast in shape: short stems of rugosa rose hips give further bright touches.

If there were no other containers available for arranging flowers we

This mixed group of late summer flowers arranged in the shallow base of an entree dish is given extra height by standing the dish on its upturned lid. The flowers are kept in position by large-mesh wire netting

A variety of possible containers for flowers outside a basket shop

A small basket suitable either for a child bridesmaid to carry or as a means of taking flowers to a hospital patient

could perhaps manage, in most circumstances, with baskets. These vary not only in shapes and sizes, but also in texture, so that there is usually something suitable, somewhere.

There are baskets made from Suffolk or Kentish reeds with a soft grey-blue-green colouring or from Norfolk willows, dark brown interlaced with pale buff; baskets in highly varnished materials, less sympathetic in outline but perhaps suggesting a more formal appearance; closely woven baskets, and ones with openwork designs, some in a large mesh and others in minutely worked patterns which almost give the feeling of fine needlework. From China there are delicate circular baskets as light as the proverbial feather, and finally in complete contrast are the sturdy, brightly coloured baskets from Andorra, in the Pyrenees.

From the point of view of flower arrangement a very important aspect of a basket is its handle. With some shapes a spreading arrangement is indicated, when the handle can become a focal point. This is most useful for twining branches, especially in the case of plants with graceful stems such as summer jasmine, hop, periwinkle and clematis. The handle should be allowed to show clearly, otherwise the shape of the basket will not be complete.

Containers holding the water must, of course, fit into the basket as neatly as possible. They may be glass cooking dishes, biscuit tins or lids, baking tins (sandwich, cake, or loaf baking tins are especially suitable), and jam jars. The tins will be less noticeable if they are painted a soft colour. This also applies to the large-mesh wire netting that will act as an anchorage to the flowers.

I think it is true to say that the colour and texture of many baskets is especially suitable for dried flowers. The colours of dried flowers are soft – there is nothing strident or unsympathetic about them – coming either in the tones and shades that are associated with a Corot or a Breughel, or in the deep velvet colours of Van Dyck, or in aubergine, tawny buffs, grey-blues, olive, off-white and pale pinks which blend well with basketwork.

The most useful of all baskets is probably the trug. A large one is invaluable for weeding or collecting cut flowers for the house, and the smaller ones for holding string, scissors, wall nails, secateurs, and all the paraphernalia required for tidying up the garden. A trug basket also makes an attractive container for holding house plants.

Many types of baskets are suitable for holding flowers to give as gifts to patients in hospital. Some are manufactured in a close white wickerwork, equipped with a green tin lining, and these come in a variety of shapes and sizes, some with handles and others without. One type is even made with a lid.

With some of the smaller posy baskets it may be better to use damp moss, Oasis or sand for the flowers than to trust to a little jar of water which can easily be spilt. But if you decide on water it is as well to fill up on arrival at the hospital so as to ensure that the basket does not drip.

As I have tried to emphasize throughout this book, one can paint with colours in flowers as one would use colours from a paintbox. This photograph shows how, by using tones of the two primary colours of red and yellow and the secondary colour of green, there becomes available a large range including bright yellow, orange, red and cream with olive green, forest green and deep blue-grey green. In this group they are introduced by many-coloured nasturtiums with their leaves, and a packet of nasturtium seeds is recommended as an investment for anyone with a decoration scheme which demands these particular colours.

Nasturtiums are not often used for indoor decoration and this may be on account of their reputation for not lasting well or because of their rather strong scent. It is also sometimes difficult to find stems long enough for cutting. But apart from the brightness of the flowers much of the beauty of this plant lies in the stems and buds and also in the many different sizes and tones of leaf. The shape of the nasturtium leaf is unusual and when looked into closely it is seen to be of fascinating design rather like a solid cobweb.

If cut when not quite fully out nasturtium flowers will generally last quite well and the leaves are definitely long-lasting. There are few plants with such a decorative habit of growth, lending themselves to generous curves and unusual patterns. They are probably at their best when arranged in a shallow dish so that one can see clearly into the flowers and the curving stems can be appreciated.

Nasturtium plants flower generously throughout the summer and go on until the harshest frosts finish them off, providing some of the last touches of bright colour in the late autumn. Their leaves will combine well with certain other flowers having little foliage of their own, such as gerberas, dwarf zinnias and love-in-a-mist – their solid roundness contrasts well with its feathery foliage – and if large leaves are cut quite short these will give a solid basis to the arrangement.

The emphasis so far has been on colour – understandably so with such a bright flower. But the shape of the group is especially important in this case and is essentially due to the porcelain vase in which the nasturtiums are arranged. Long, sturdy stems are given some support from wire netting, but the depth of the vase gives them extra strength.

Sometimes the shape or texture or colour of a vase will, as much as the flowers, indicate the type of arrangement most suitable for the required occasion. If it will also, by its shape, give a variety of positions, then so much the better. Such a vase is an economy and provides an answer to people who feel that a large selection of containers is essential when doing flower arrangements in their home. I have always felt that this is a mistaken idea and I think it will be found that even if one has a number of different vases there are always one or two which become favourites and which are used most frequently.

Both the shape and colouring of this porcelain jar is particularly suitable for the nasturtiums. The narrow neck gives extra support to the stems which are also kept in position towards the centre by wire netting

This white cornucopia illustrates many useful points. It looks equally well with either a few or several flowers, and being white, will fit in with any colour scheme. It holds plenty of water and encourages an arrangement of graceful shape. The three arum lilies are another example of using an uneven number of flowers when there are only a few to be arranged

When looking round for a versatile vase it is important to select one which will fit into almost any colour scheme, be simple to arrange, and capable of taking a sizeable group without necessitating the use of too many flowers – a valuable economy in the winter months.

A white arrangement can be suitable to so many situations that often the most truly versatile vase will be a white one.

As this particular vase is rather unusual in shape, a more ordinary design might be easier to find. But it appears that whatever is selected should be open – that is, with a wide neck. For instance, whereas a wine decanter or a champagne glass might not be suitable, a cornucopia, a large shell, or a basket would probably all be possible.

The arum lily featured in this arrangement is not as delicate as it is often thought to be. Like most plants, it dislikes a draught. It seems to prefer a sunny, well-drained position, but I have also known of it growing along the water's edge. In my own garden it is close to water but not actually in it, and its roots must, I feel sure, reach the moisture during dry weather, which it seems to like. I protect it during the winter months with dried bracken. The point about growing it right in the water is to protect the roots during severe frost, but I have not yet had the courage to try this and as my plants seem happy as they are I shall not do so unless it becomes necessary. They flourish at the moment as they are, and I am grateful for that.

Index

Page numbers in italics denote illustrations